THE STIG

THE UNTOLD STORY

This book contains adult humour and
some themes that may be unsuitable for children.

THE STIG

THE UNTOLD STORY

Simon du Beaumarche

1 3 5 7 9 10 8 6 4 2

Published in 2012 by BBC Books, an imprint of Ebury Publishing
A Random House Group company

This book is intended as a humorous work of fiction. Whilst it features some real people,
it also features made-up people, and stuff that didn't actually happen.

The Random House Group Limited Reg. 954009

Addresses for companies within the Random House Group can be found at
www.randomhouse.co.uk

A CIP catalogue record for this book is available from the British Library

Hardback ISBN 978 1 84 990540 4
Trade paperback ISBN 978 1 84 990579 4

The Random House Group Limited supports The Forest Stewardship Council® (FSC®),
the leading international forest certification organisation. Our books carrying the FSC label
and printed on FSC® certified paper. FSC is the only forest certification scheme endorsed
by leading environmental organisations, including Greenpeace. Our paper
procurement policy can be found at www.randomhouse.co.uk

Typeset by seagulls.net
Printed and bound in England by Clays Ltd, St Ives plc

To buy books by your favourite authors and register for offers, visit www.randomhouse.co.uk

Picture credits

BBC Books would like to thank the following individuals and organisations
for providing photographs and for permission to reproduce copyright material.
While every effort has been made to trace and acknowledge copyright holders,
we would like to apologise should there be any errors or omissions.

Section 1: Alistair Berg p7 (main); Bettmann/Corbis p2; Hulton-Deutsch Collection/
Corbis p6 (bottom); Mirrorpix p6 (top); Phipps/Sutton Images/Corbis p4 (top), p5;
Press Association Images p8 ; Rex Features p1, p3 (top), p4 (bottom),
p7 (detail); Schlegelmilch/Corbis p3 (bottom)

Section 2: Alison Jackson Studios, www.alisonjackson.com p1-6; Mikhail Kondrashov
"fotomik"/Alamy p7 (main); Noel Yates/Alamy p8 (top); Rex Features p7 (detail);
Robert Brook/Alamy p8 (bottom)

CONTENTS

INTRODUCTION

When my agent first approached me to write this biography, I must confess to a sense of trepidation. With acclaimed works such as *Kylie Minogue: Little & Lucky*, *Katie Price: Making Some Boobs* and the best-selling work *Touching Princess Anne*, I certainly had experience of writing biographies, but I was also concerned that it would be extremely difficult to profile a man who never spoke.

Yet it was this very mystery that also drew me to this project, just as it seems to draw people to The Stig in general. Indeed, 'Who is The Stig?' is one of the most popular internet searches in the world, vastly outnumbering other popular *Top Gear*-related searches such as, 'What is Jeremy Clarkson?', 'Where is Richard Hammond?' and 'Why is James May?' It seems the world's fascination with the so-called 'tame racing driver' knows no bounds.

As a biographer, the question, 'Who is The Stig?' goes deeper than simply putting a name and a face to the person behind the reflective mask. It's about unearthing who he really is, discovering what makes him tick and finding the truth behind rumours such as a claim that he once ate an entire jar of Nutella in one sitting (I checked this one thoroughly and, yes, it seems that he did, including the lid).

I knew this could not be a conventional biography. There would be no progression through being born in the Republic of Ireland, moving to the UK at a young age, struggling to be accepted and lose an unfamiliar accent then getting a break in a tough industry and steadily climbing the ladder to become a star. If you're looking for that, might I humbly recommend my best-selling work on Des Lynam, *Badger of Honour*.

The Stig is not a conventional man, and that will be reflected in my work. However, as I embark on this task – with the promise of co-operation from the BBC and *Top Gear* itself – I hope to find things that you have never heard before, and that from these remarkable tales we will all be able to glean a little more about the man, the legend, the internet search phenomenon that is The Stig.

Simon du Beaumarche

London

1

SOME SAY...

The origins of The Stig are a great mystery. Where does he come from? Where is he going to? What made him into a speechless speed machine? Why did a well-known member of the *Top Gear* team warn me not to approach him from the left-hand side unless I wanted to be 'literally drenched'?

If you watch the *Top Gear* television programme regularly, there are several things you will know with some certainty about The Stig. He is a supremely fast and talented driver. He steadfastly refuses to speak. He has a taste in music that could be filed under anything from 'eclectic' to 'extremely strange'.

Those are the enduring and familiar qualities, the things that come up time and again, but there are other clear aspects of his character that can be observed if you spend an entire week at home, as I did, watching endless episodes of *Top Gear* back to back until you completely lose your mind and are discovered wandering through a local park repeatedly mumbling, 'Meanwhile ...' under your breath. The Stig appears to be genuinely confused by and/or fearful of stairs. He has a real issue with Scouts. He seems capable of obeying basic instructions but when he decides something is not to his liking there is every chance he will simply walk off.

Then there are the aspects of The Stig's character alluded to in the TV show's famous, 'Some say ...' introductions. Are they grounded in reality or mere flights of fancy to distract from the already complex character behind the tinted visor? As a biographer, I have often discovered that the biggest clues to a subject's life are the most obvious and, with that in mind, I took the liberty of cross-checking some of the things that have been claimed about The Stig in those humorous studio lines. Here are some of the things I discovered:

Some say ... there's an airport in Russia named after him. I have checked this and the answer is no, there isn't. It's a heliport, and this could be a coincidence.

Some say ... he's allergic to the Dutch. Unlikely, since this is not a documented medical condition. The doctors I consulted said sudden exposure to the Dutch might bring on, at most, some light sneezing and a superficial skin rash.

Some say ... he once had a vicious knife fight with the television presenter, Anthea Turner. Difficult to prove. A spokesperson for Ms Turner said she has been in 'many vicious knife fights, and it would be impossible for her to remember all of her adversaries'.

Some say ... he's banned from the town of Chichester. The police in the town confirm that this is not true. The ban was lifted in 2004, though he cannot go back to the fireplace shop.

Some say ... he invented the curtain. In theory not out of the question, but only if you believe Wikipedia, which claims that the curtain was invented in 1992.

Some say ... there are seventeen reasons why he is banned from the Northampton branch of Little Chef. I telephoned the Northampton branch of Little Chef and they confirmed that this is wrong. There are only nine reasons. Eight if you accept that he was basically doing the same thing with the gravy and the custard.

Some say ... he once punched a horse to the ground. Quite hard to prove, either way. It would certainly take some effort, depending on the size of the horse.

It seemed clear that the 'Some say ...' lines erred on the side of whimsy or exaggeration. The real truths about The Stig lay somewhere else, and it would be my job to find them.

It seemed logical to start with the story of how The Stig came to be on *Top Gear*. Former BBC development producer, Simon Fotherington, is one of the people credited with bringing the programme back to our screens in 2002, and he remembers well the moment The Stig arrived on the scene: 'We knew we wanted to have a test track and that we wanted a racing driver to set lap times,' Fotherington recalls, pacing around his office at Soft Cheese Media where he is now senior creative executive director of production. 'We'd organised a day of auditions down at Dunsfold [location of the *Top Gear* airfield] and got a few pro drivers down. They were all pretty good, I guess, but then at the end of the day, as we were packing up, something really weird happened ...'

CHAPTER ONE

Fotherington sits down in the high-backed leather swivel chair behind his desk and leans forward, his eyes full of intensity.

'I mean, really weird,' he says, softly. 'It's a pretty warm evening, right, but all of a sudden the air just goes cold. Not from the wind – the temperature just literally drops and the whole place seems to go deadly quiet, like that sensation you get just before a storm. Then, from across the other side of the airfield, this massive flock of crows comes flying towards us, really low and really slow and just as they get overhead they start making this unholy racket and then just disappear over the buildings. It was strange. Really strange. So we were all looking at each other, and I remember a few of us actually shivered a bit, and we started packing up as fast as we could because ... I can't really explain, but it was spooky, when suddenly from behind us there's this furious revving and, when we look round, there's this guy just sitting in the BMW we'd been using on the track, stopped perfectly on the start line, just revving and revving the engine.'

For a brief moment Fotherington's eyes seem to glaze over and he looks slightly hollow and scared. Almost immediately, he snaps himself out of his trance.

'My first reaction was to be a bit embarrassed,' he recalls. 'You know, we thought we'd somehow forgotten one of the drivers we were supposed to be testing so we didn't say anything to this chap; we just got the stopwatch out and set him off. Before you know it, he's back again and he's *three seconds* faster than anyone else we've seen that day. What's really amazing is that we'd never even shown him the track layout; he just worked it out on his first lap, and he was *still* the fastest.'

However, Fotherington recalls that the strange newcomer's ability in front of the camera was nowhere near as impressive as his driving.

'We set up the camera again and handed him the rough script we'd written for the day,' the former development producer recalls, removing his thick-framed glasses and wiping them idly on his shirt. 'Well, he just threw it on the floor, which was pretty surprising. Then we stood him in front of the camera and the director shouted "ACTION!" What happened next was ... nothing. Not a word. He just stood there. I remember telling him to take his time, just go when he was ready – all that sort of thing. And still he just stood there, arms folded, helmet on, not saying a word. In fact, we hadn't heard him speak once since he'd arrived.'

At this point, things became even stranger for Fotherington and his team.

'The director suggested we take a minute and we stopped rolling the camera,' he remembers. 'At which point, one of our production assistants came over with her list of auditionees, looking a bit confused. "We don't know who this guy is," I remember her saying. "He's definitely not on the list." She said he must have just, you know, *turned up*. It was really random.'

Proceedings then took a turn for the worse, according to Fotherington.

'The director didn't know we'd got some wild card here and before I had time to say anything, he called for the camera to start turning again so we could try for a take. He said something to this mystery guy about taking his crash helmet off and then delivering his lines, and at this point the guy just walks off. Doesn't speak, and then just strolls off. It was like working with Keith Floyd all over again.'

The *Top Gear* team were left baffled by the mystery driver, but thought no more of it until they were back in the programme's London office, at which point someone mentioned this strange moment to presenter, Jeremy Clarkson.

'Quite unexpectedly, Jeremy was *very* excited by this story,' Fotherington recalls. 'I remember him pacing about the room recapping what he'd just been told. "He's incredibly fast but he doesn't speak? This is BRILLIANT!" I remember him saying. And then he started saying how this was the perfect thing for the programme because, "*literally* no-one is interested" in anything racing drivers have to say.'

The fast-but-silent driver's place on the new programme was assured and Clarkson decided he would be called 'The Gimp'. The BBC, however, weren't so sure.

'I got called into a top-level meeting of all the big chiefs on the sixth floor of Television Centre,' Fotherington recounts. 'They were all there. Jane, Sarah, Alice, Jane, Jane, Jane and Jane. They told me that under no circumstances would the BBC allow a prime-time programme to feature a character called "The Gimp". That gave us a bit of a problem, 'cos we were about to shoot the pilot episode. We'd lured this mystery chap back to the track by leaving a powerful Lamborghini on the start line and, when he showed up, we'd invited him into our Portakabin and given him a room of his own for some privacy. Well, he went in there and there was a hell of a lot of banging behind the closed door. At one point it turned into a pretty frightening screeching, sort of like badly maintained train brakes and angry foxes mating at the same time, but eventually he came out. He'd left behind one hell of a mess – Ribena literally everywhere, and scratched into the paint on one wall was what looked like a single word: "STIG". Since we couldn't think of anything else, that just sort of became his name. When he was asked about it later, Jeremy claimed the name came from what they used to call new boys at his school, but I know for a fact that at Jeremy's school the new boys were called "bumholes".'

With the addition of a definite article to the front, *Top Gear* had its new in-house racing driver. He was called The Stig.

Having established how he came to appear on the programme, my next step was to watch him at work.

2

AT THE TOP GEAR STUDIO

At dawn on a cold, icy day in February, the *Top Gear* test track is a desolate place. A chill wind whips across the former airfield, cutting through clothing and cooling the blood of any living creature, whilst signally failing to shift the cap of grey cloud that sits gloomily above the steely grey tarmac.

The *Top Gear* production offices are barely less bleak: a cluster of tatty Portakabins cobbled together to make a series of stark and inadequately furnished rooms, each one less inviting than the last. There is a conspicuously inadequate amount of furniture and what little there is falls into one of two categories, being either old or broken. At one point, I go to sit on a tattered stool in the corner that goes from being the former to being the latter as soon as I put my weight on it. A helpful member of the production team helps me to my feet and thoughtfully tells me that the sticky mess I have fallen into is most likely just a mixture of spilt Fanta and mouse poo.

The *Top Gear* team are here to film the studio and track segments for the fifth programme in their eighteenth series. I had been told to arrive early if I wanted to watch The Stig in action. 'We're summoning him to the track today using Method 4F,' one of the producers tells me. 'It's the one with the lamb shanks on a lazy Susan.' This, I was later informed, is one of several ways in which The Stig can be drawn to the airfield so that he might undertake his *Top Gear* duties. I was intending to ask if I could see this process in action but I was too late: at just after 8.30 a.m., there he was, a figure in white striding down the start/finish straight, relaxed and yet purposeful, striking and fascinating. He turned off the track itself, through the open gate in the large wire fence and across the *Top Gear* compound. He passed me as I stood by one of the film crew's vans, and I thought for a moment I detected a faint smell of lychees.

At a respectful distance, I followed The Stig as he walked around the production building and up a shallow ramp that led to the rear entrance. He walked straight in, past a foul-smelling kitchen area and strode through a door marked 'STIG'S ROOM', which he closed immediately behind him. As I approached the door a member of the production team lightly grabbed my arm. 'Do you like blood?' she asked. I said that I was not especially keen. 'Do you like searing amounts of pain and spending weeks being unable to shake off the smell of moussaka?'

I laughed at her seemingly bizarre line of questioning.

'Sorry,' she continued. 'I don't mean to be rude, it's just that I wouldn't go in there right now unless you really, *really* like all of those things. Do you see what I mean?' I did.

I walked outside and waited for The Stig to re-emerge. Sure enough, at just before 9 a.m., he came briskly across the car park and walked straight to the Maserati already positioned on the start line, getting into the car and starting the engine in one smooth, seamless movement. A producer leant in through the open door and said something to The Stig that I was too far away to catch. The door closed, there was a brief pause and then the Maserati screeched away from the line with a blare of exhaust noise. Was that a brief smell of hessian I detected? It was hard to tell.

'He's just going out to get his eye in,' the producer explained to me. 'One or two laps to get a feel for the car, and then he'll really start banging them in. He's usually pretty fast on his first hot lap; after that, we're just chipping away a tenth or two. If the lap times ever go up rather than down, we know something's seriously wrong. We haul him in, give him a single After Eight mint and show him a picture of Dame Judi Dench. That's usually enough, but if he's *really* not on song, we've got a DVD of *'Allo 'Allo* and the special tea towels on stand by …'

I was about to ask what would be done with these unusually paired items to motivate the star driver but the producer then indicated that he had to keep an eye on the stopwatch and turned away to face the track.

For over an hour, I watched The Stig lapping first the Maserati and then a high-powered Mercedes. In all that time he showed no emotion and no interest in anything except driving the cars and driving them fast. At one point, as he switched between cars, a photographer from the *Top Gear* website asked him to pose for some pictures. The Stig stood still for, at most, ten seconds. Then, without prompting, he simply walked off, got into the Mercedes and reversed it onto the start line ready to do another lap, leaving the photographer spluttering, 'But I wasn't finished ...'

Eventually, the producer advised me that the *Top Gear* presenters had arrived and now would be a good time to introduce myself, before they started rehearsals. I was ushered back to the offices. From the cars parked outside I could deduce that Jeremy Clarkson had arrived in his black Mercedes, Richard Hammond had arrived in his grey Porsche and James May had not arrived at all. A researcher explained that he had set off from home and then had to go back because he had forgotten his trousers.

I was led through to the presenters' green room at the back of the Portakabin. It was a bare space containing three ill-matched sofas, a tiny desk with a computer on it and a small fridge that may have once been white. The room was dominated by the sound of a man shouting: 'I bet he'd forgotten to put them on, the ridiculous arse.' The man stopped talking and looked at me. It was Jeremy Clarkson. Introductions were made and I went to sit down on a spare sofa.

'I wouldn't sit there,' Clarkson exclaimed.

'Yeah, I really wouldn't sit there,' Hammond added. 'It's *very* damp. Been like that for weeks – no idea why.'

Clarkson lit a cigarette and flicked idly at a pile of newspapers on the seat next to him. 'So,' he exhaled. 'A biography? Where do you want to start?'

My mind was still somewhat preoccupied by the mysterious room I had seen The Stig disappear into earlier. Would it be possible, I asked, to have a look inside?

Hammond spluttered and then pretended to look intently at a copy of *Autocar* magazine. Clarkson craned his head to see out of the window behind me. 'He's still out on track,' the curly-haired presenter muttered. 'Right, let's make this quick. Hammond, keep an eye out for Stig coming back.'

'And what am I going to do? *Stop* him?' muttered Hammond, indignantly. 'Not after last time. In the end, I had to throw those trousers away.'

Clarkson led me through the shabby production offices and straight to the door of The Stig's room, at which point he paused, took a deep breath and then purposefully pushed it open. He jerked his head to indicate that I should enter.

Inside there was a cheap office table, an office chair, a patchwork of missing carpet tiles and a bean bag that had been sliced open. It smelt musty and strange. In truth, there was little to distinguish it from all the other rooms in the *Top Gear* production centre. Clarkson appeared to register my disappointment. 'Look more closely,' he said, quietly. 'Look at the walls.'

I did. They were covered in what could only be scratch marks, made by a human-sized hand. Where, I asked, had these come from?

'Who knows?' Clarkson shrugged, extinguishing his cigarette and lighting another one. 'It'll be no different for months and then suddenly there'll be a load more. All sorts of things seem to trigger it. Pictures of the new Dodge Viper. News of Tim Henman's retirement. The time they bought out Reggae-Reggae-sauce-flavoured crisps. We're not sure if it's a good thing or a bad thing. The scratches I mean, not the crisps. The crisps are quite nice.'

I surveyed the rest of the room more closely. On a low table in the corner sat a cheap portable television with 'Property of Novotel Hammersmith' stencilled on the side. Next to it was a DVD player and a pile of DVD cases. I flicked through them: *Love Actually*, *Born Free*, *The Railway Children*, *Terms of Endearment*, *Love Story*, *Straw Dogs*, and *Brief Encounter*. Two discs were lying out on their own without cases: the Bette Midler weepie, *Beaches*, and orangutan-based hotel comedy, *Dunston Checks In*.

'He leaves an Amazon film list outside the door with crosses against the stuff he wants and we get them for him,' Clarkson explained. 'It's the same with the music he listens to when he's driving. No-one's quite sure how he's getting access to the internet in the first place. As far as we know, he doesn't have a computer.'

At that moment, a familiar voice could be heard outside the door. 'I didn't forget to put on my bloody trousers, you clot,' it said peevishly. 'I'd forgotten my *other* trousers to wear for the recording.' It seemed James May was here.

A COMPLETE LIST OF THE ITEMS OBSERVED IN THE STIG'S ROOM

- 9 x DVDs (see main text)
- 1 x portable television (stolen)
- 1 x DVD player (sticky)
- 1 x copy *How To Be The Perfect Housewife* by Anthea Turner
- 1 x poster of Norwegian pop band A-Ha (crumpled)
- 2 x tins of Spam
- 1 x rare 1980s Jasper Carrott action doll
- 1 x owner's manual for a hot air balloon
- 12 x sections of Scalextric track
- 2 x Scalextric cars (chewed)
- 1 x packet of *Happy Mutt!* dog treats (unopened)
- 1 x packet of *Happy Mutt!* dog treats (opened)
- 1 x packet of *Happy Mutt!* dog treats (almost unrecognisable)
- 1 x Post-It note with 'CALL BIGGINS' written on it.

'Let me get this straight,' another voice said. It was Richard Hammond. 'You pooed your pants and had to go home again ...'

Clarkson stepped smartly from The Stig's room. 'Morning, May,' he boomed. 'Left the house without your trousers again ...?'

From outside, May harrumphed and muttered something about 'being fatuous'. Clarkson stuck his head back into the room. 'We have a rehearsal to do,' he said, matter-of-factly. 'If I were you, I'd get out of here before Stig comes back.'

I did as Clarkson suggested. Out on the track, the week's celebrity guest had arrived. It was *Doctor Who* star, Matt Smith. I was going to suggest that he could one day become the subject of a best-selling biography, just as his predecessor, Tom Baker, had with my acclaimed work, *Who's Bonkers Now?*, but thought better of it. Instead, I carefully observed how The Stig worked to coach a track-driving novice in the famous Reasonably Priced Car.

Strangely, for a man who had earlier shown little patience, The Stig seemed calm and easy-going. He drove Smith around the track twice, accompanied him as a passenger for three laps and then let him get on with it, occasionally approaching the car as it came to a stop after a fast lap and poking his head through the window. At one point, he wandered off to a distant expanse of grass and stood stock-still with his back to the track. Three crows landed in unison in front of him and The Stig stared at them for several minutes. No-one else appeared to notice this or, if they did, they seemed utterly unconcerned by it.

When Smith had finished his laps I managed to ask him what The Stig had said to him during his time on the track.

'Not a lot, really,' the actor admitted. 'Gestures mostly, a few clicks, a sort of low hum. I think he did say, "Brake here" at one point and something else that sounded like "Omnislice", but really not a whole lot.'

Nonetheless, Smith must be one of the few people in the world to have heard The Stig speak. What did it sound like?

'Firm but soft. Like having two high-quality pillows rubbed on the side of your head,' the *Doctor Who* star mused. 'I think he might be Welsh. Or Scottish. Or maybe French. It's hard to tell, really. What's that country next to Malaysia? You know, *thingy*. I'm pretty sure he's not from there.'

After lunch, the audience filed into the *Top Gear* hangar and the afternoon's recording began. There was no sign of The Stig. I found James May in a quiet corner of the building, waiting for the cameras and the assembled crowd to be positioned for the next link. As we waited, I asked him if The Stig ever came into the studio and mingled with the audience.

'Not any more,' the floppy-haired presenter replied. 'Too many people got hurt last time.'

In which case, what did The Stig do whilst the studio recording was in progress? May shrugged and took a deep swig from his mug of tea.

'No-one really knows,' he whispered. 'He just sort of disappears off to his ... well, wherever it is he lives, I suppose. We're not entirely sure. Funnily enough, a few series ago one of our researchers followed him as he left the studio. Stig wandered off towards the far side of the airfield and she tailed him as far as where the trees start over on the south side ... or north side ... basically, that side over there, and that's the last she remembers. Next thing she knew, she woke up inside an industrial dustbin behind an Asda in Burnley. Or Lincoln. One of the two. All rather peculiar ...'

A floor manager approached us and informed James that they were now ready to record the next studio link.

'I'm so sorry,' May said, graciously. 'I have to go and do some speaking on camera. It's my job, you see …' and with that he disappeared into the crowd.

As the cameras rolled, I slipped out of the back door of the studio, walked towards the production offices and stood by a cluster of parked cars hoping to spot The Stig so that I might pursue him as he left the premises. As luck would have it, just two or three minutes later he came striding purposefully past the shabby Portakabin offices so, maintaining a safe distance, I started to follow him as he walked down the side of the building and turned smartly right at the end of the path, disappearing behind another old hanger. As he disappeared from view I stepped up my pace and made the same turn. That was the last thing that I remember.

I woke up some 20 hours later in a barn near Stoke-on-Trent with absolutely no idea how I had got there or how I would get home (the answer to the latter turned out to be unfriendly farmer/more friendly farmer/taxi/train/taxi).

It was a strange and unsettling experience that I would not wish to repeat in a hurry. Worse still, it gave me a worrying sense that tracking down the truth about The Stig was going to be even harder than I had first feared. At least, however, I had my next tactic mapped out: I was going to talk to some of those who should know him best.

3

JEREMY CLARKSON ON THE STIG

Few have spent more time with The Stig than the *Top Gear* presenters themselves. It therefore seemed logical to assume that if anyone knew anything about this elusive character it would be these three and, happily, each had agreed to give me a one-to-one interview about their so-called 'tame racing driver'. My first chat would be with Jeremy Clarkson.

One week after my first trip to the *Top Gear* track, the presenter invited me to visit the Surrey facility again and agreed that he would talk to me in a break from filming a Lamborghini sports car for his forthcoming DVD release, *Everything Just Literally Exploded*.

When I arrived at Dunsfold, the security guard at the gate pointed me in the right direction: 'Just follow the noise of screaming engines,' he said, cheerily. 'When the smell of burning rubber gets a bit much, you'll know you're there!'

Sure enough, as I reached the edge of the old airstrip, I pointed my rented car towards what appeared to be a thick, ever-expanding cloud in the middle of the runway, and was almost at its feathery fringes when a rakish yellow supercar burst from within and skidded to a halt next to a film crew leaning on a black van. As the car stopped, a cameraman slid off the bonnet.

Clarkson clambered from the driver's seat, a freshly ignited cigarette already in his mouth. 'Sorry about that, Dave,' he boomed, as his errant colleague picked himself up from the ground. 'I didn't realise you'd be that close. That's going to make a GREAT shot. And you're not bleeding as much as I expected. Good!'

I re-introduced myself to Clarkson and he invited me to step into the Italian supercar for the short trip across the airfield to the *Top Gear* production offices, where we could sit down and chat.

'A classic moment!' the presenter boomed as I struggled to do up my seat belt. 'I LITERALLY just killed a cameraman! AGAIN!' I was about to point out that, miraculously, the man appeared to be very much alive, but then Clarkson started the powerful engine and accelerated violently.

A few smoky seconds later we were at the offices and, once I had finished being sick, Jeremy invited me to step inside the shabby Portakabins so we could talk.

'Do you smoke?' Jeremy said as he sparked another Marlboro Light. 'No? You should. Did you know that 92 per cent of all the great inventors smoked? It's true. And if you smoke, your kids won't have ginger hair. Something to do with a chemical in them. I met this smoking expert in France when I was filming *Funny Foreigners On The Limit* back in the nineties, and he literally knew everything about fags. I'd love to get him on the show but he's busy. Or dead. I can't remember which.'

We sat down in a room festooned with pictures of star guests out on the test track, many of them posing with The Stig himself. I accepted Clarkson's offer of a coffee and he disappeared off towards the kitchen area. For a few minutes all was quiet before the silence was broken by manic banging and muffled swearing, the tortured howl of metal screeching against metal and, finally, the sound of breaking glass.

Clarkson thundered back into the room. 'There's something wrong with the coffee machine,' he exclaimed. 'You can have one of these.' He tossed me a can of Red Bull, opened one for himself, lit a cigarette and sat down on the sofa opposite. 'Right!' he bellowed. 'Where are you up to with this book?'

I outlined my quest thus far to find the truth about The Stig, about where he came from and what made him into the man he is today, and explained that talking to those closest to a person can supply vital information that the subject themselves may be unwilling or unable to provide. As a fine example of this, I cited the work I did for my acclaimed biography of the musician, Prince: *Purple Pain*.

As my explanation came to an end, Clarkson said nothing for a moment. Eventually, the silence was broken by the sound of a Red Bull can being opened and a lighter being applied to the end of a cigarette. The presenter exhaled slowly and leaned forward.

'So, in essence, you want to know where The Stig came from?' he said, carefully. 'Well, you're in luck, because I know *exactly* where he came from ...'

Clarkson took another long drag on his cigarette and fixed me with his slightly blood-shot eyes.

'I warn you now, this will blow your socks off,' he continued. He tapped a grey cylinder of spent ash into his already-drained Red Bull can and cleared his throat.

'You know the top-secret military base in the Nevada desert where the US government supposedly keeps all the alien life forms that have visited Earth? They call it Area 51. But what you won't find on Wikipedia is that there was another base next to it. It was called Area 52.'

A member of the film crew entered the room holding a small cup. 'We've got the spare coffee machine working,' he said. 'Triple espresso, okay?'

Clarkson received the powerful coffee with thanks and drank it in one go. 'Top man,' he said, as he gulped. 'Can someone get me another Red Bull, too? Many thanks.'

I asked him to continue with his explanation of Area 52.

'Yes, Area 52. If you think Area 51 is secret, you have literally no idea how secret this place was. It was a series of massive concrete bunkers, about two miles underground, all run by the military. But the lab rats in this place weren't aliens – they were humans.'

As Clarkson let me digest this remarkable claim, another member of the crew arrived with a four-pack of Red Bull. The presenter cracked another can with one hand whilst lighting a cigarette, and continued: 'What you must understand is that this was built in the 1960s, literally the height of the Cold War. Everyone was paranoid that the Russians would invade, and so the military had literally millions, no, billions, no, wait, what's the one above that? They had literally squillions of dollars to spend on coming up with new weapons. Have you heard of The Virtus Project?'

I confessed that I hadn't.

'The Virtus Project was what went on at Area 52,' Clarkson stated, through a thick cloud of smoke. 'The military scientists there, they came up with this special serum that made ordinary soldiers into super-soldiers. Obviously it made some of them stronger and tougher, but what was special about this serum was that it could be tailored to target and enhance specific skills. Some soldiers had massive lungs and could swim really fast underwater. Others had hugely expanded brains and were trained as technical spies who could literally photograph everything in an enemy weapons base using just their eyes. And then there was another group. A group that was given ultra-fast reactions.'

Clarkson paused both for dramatic effect and to light a cigarette.

'The serum was tailored precisely for them by adding the DNA of fighter pilots, racing drivers, cobras, leopards, mongooses, more leopards, certain sorts of badger. Basically, anybody or anything with lightning reactions. And the results were astonishing. Once injected, these men could literally slow down time. Things happening at 200 m.p.h., to their brains, seemed like they were happening at 20.'

I could see where this was going and asked Clarkson to continue.

'The serum worked well, but it also had side effects. When it remapped their nervous systems, the serum also destroyed the part of the brain that deals with feelings and emotions. This particular group became literally ... robots.'

The silence in the room was deafening. It was broken by the sound of a Red Bull can being opened.

'Now the thing is,' Clarkson continued with gusto, 'the military couldn't let any of this get out. If the public heard they were turning real people into zombies there'd have been an outcry and the whole Virtus programme would have been shut down. So the top generals decided the only thing they could do was dispose of them. All of them. But one of the soldiers – the serum hadn't quite destroyed all of his emotions. It left him with just enough feeling to understand what had happened to him and his group. He realised what was going on and organised a breakout. Now, they're escaping from a maximum security, top-secret base, and that's not easy. There are airlocks and lasers and remotely activated machine guns going off. Many of the super-soldiers were killed as they tried to escape, but a handful did get away.'

Clarkson paused to wipe away the Red Bull that he'd spilled on his shirt whilst miming remotely activated machine gun fire.

'So now they're fugitives, on the run from a military that desperately wants to hunt them down and destroy them. The only thing they can do to survive is go to ground, literally vanishing from the face of the earth.'

I had to ask the obvious question: where did The Stig fit into all this?

'It's simple,' Clarkson replied, lighting another cigarette. 'The Stig is him. The leader. The one who broke them out. His reactions are what make him drive like he does, and now he's hiding out here, on *Top Gear*. Nobody sees his face, nobody hears him speak.'

I had to point out the obvious flaw in this theory: The Stig is seen on TV all the time, and known all around the world as a result. That hardly seemed like hiding.

'That's the beauty of it,' Clarkson exclaimed. 'The best way of hiding is to be completely visible, but invisible. It's a *double* double bluff. It also explains the bizarre music choices in the car. His brain is searching for fragments of his past so he can work out who he is. So he tries easy listening, then Country and Western, then foreign language tapes and so on.'

Another obvious question was, if we knew where the leader was, what had happened to all the other escaped supermen?

'I knew you'd ask that,' Clarkson roared. 'And where do you think The Stig's cousins come from? African cousin, Chinese cousin, American cousin ... that's *them*.'

At that moment, the director appeared in the doorway and reminded Jeremy that they needed to carry on with filming.

Clarkson stood up and cracked another can of Red Bull. 'Right,' he shouted as he took a swig. 'Back to the playground.'

He rummaged in his bag, pulling out another pack of cigarettes and his iPad. 'Oh, for the love of God,' he muttered, jabbing at its touch-sensitive screen. 'James May has just e-mailed me an explanation of active aerodynamics. I literally don't have the 50 *million* years I'd need to read it.'

He tossed the iPad onto the sofa, next to me.

'Here,' he boomed. 'See if you can understand literally one word of that.'

With that, Clarkson was gone. I picked up the iPad and began to scan the e-mail from James May. It was, indeed, rather technical and wordy. Some of it appeared to be in Latin. The production offices were suddenly very quiet. I stood up and went to put the iPad back into Clarkson's voluminous bag on the other sofa. As I did so, I noticed that inside was a small collection of DVDs: *The Bourne Trilogy*, a series of films about a man whose mind is controlled by a secret department of the US government; *Captain America*, the Hollywood blockbuster about a super-soldier created by a secret department of the government; and *Universal Soldier*, the Jean-Claude Van Damme classic about a super-soldier created by a secret department of the government.

I thought back to the last hour's conversation with Clarkson and a chill ran down my spine. Had I just sat through a carefully crafted script drawn from these films? Was this some clever plot to throw outsiders off the scent of The Stig? Had Jeremy Clarkson been lying to me?

It would be easy to think so. However, I have interviewed enough people over the years to know when someone isn't telling the truth, and I got no sense of that here. Jeremy's words smelt of sincerity. And cigarettes.

The only conclusion I could draw was that Clarkson really believed this stuff. Maybe he had driven through one too many brick walls.

4

JAMES MAY ON THE STIG

'Oh, Clarkson's definitely driven through too many brick walls, all right,' said a warm, familiar voice from beneath an unruly thatch of Oscar-Wilde-meets-Prog-Rock hair. 'Did he give you his theory about super-soldiers? Thought so. The man's a halfwit.'

It was the day after Jeremy Clarkson had given me his frankly deranged super-soldiers theory about The Stig, and I was now speaking to the man they call 'Captain Slow', in the sizeable garage-cum-workshop attached to (and rather larger than) his house. After the disappointment of Clarkson's Red Bull-fuelled rantings, my hope was that the most thoughtful and academic member of the *Top Gear* trio would be able to shed a sensible light on the origins of The Stig.

The sound of a traditional kettle whistling came from the kitchen next door. 'Ah. Excuse me for a moment, the tea's ready,' May said, eagerly. Dressed in his purple and pink striped jumper, jeans and a pair of immaculately polished work boots, he got up, then paused for a moment to correct himself.

'Actually, that's not strictly correct. What I should have said was that the water from which the infusion will be made is ready. I have to add the tea. And, in due course, the milk and then, where applicable, the sugar.'

May ambled off into the kitchen, leaving me alone to take in his workshop. On the floor in the middle of the room was an old motorbike that had been stripped down and was clearly undergoing a rebuild. However, the floor looked more like the scene of an archaeological dig. All the parts were laid out with immaculate symmetry and labelled with handwritten tags. I read the nearest tag which said, 'Alternator. Removed at 09.47 GMT. Pre-inspection complete.'

On the walls, the sets of sockets and spanners were arranged in order of size, each one defined by a pencil-drawn outline of its shape on the wall behind it. The pencil used to draw the outline was itself fixed to the wall, with a pencil drawing of its shape around it to mark its place. Underneath was the Dymo-taped caption: 'HB pencil for marking the outline of wall-hung tools.' Next to it was another pencil, with the caption reading: 'HB pencil used for marking the outline of the pencil used for marking the outline of the wall-hung tools.'

Next to that was another pencil with the caption: 'HB pencil used for marking the outline of the pencil used for marking the outline of the pencil used for marking the outline of the wall-hung tools.' And so the line of pencils continued along the wall.

I managed to count almost 30 of them before I was distracted by May returning.

'Here we go, a refreshing pot of tea,' he announced, setting down a tray containing teapot, mugs and a plate of Rich Tea biscuits.

'You can dunk your biscuit if you like,' May muttered, as he poured the tea through a strainer to catch the leaves. 'But if you do, would you mind doing it when I'm not looking? I get a bit on edge if the dunked part of the Rich Tea actually falls in the tea.'

The incipient obsessive–compulsive disorder issues portrayed on *Top Gear* were clearly no television confection, but this would surely prove a bonus when it came to relaying details about The Stig. Plus, whatever May had to say, it couldn't be any worse than Clarkson's bizarre theory.

'So, yes, sorry about Jeremy and his super-soldier theory,' May began, carefully taking a biscuit from the plate. 'But that's Jezza for you, I'm afraid. He's not exactly ... I'm so sorry, but the tail-end of your watch strap has escaped from the small leather loop that would normally retain it against the inner strap and I'm finding it extremely distracting. Would you mind awfully ...?'

I tucked my errant watch strap back into place and May continued: 'Yes, well, Clarkson is a bit of a berk but I fear he genuinely believes his super-soldier theory. It's all codswallop, of course, but it keeps him distracted and stops him setting fire to things again, the cretinous oaf. Now, if you want to know where The Stig *really* comes from, I'm pleased to say I can tell you.'

The shaggy-haired presenter paused. The pause became an actual silence. The silence seemed to last for an interminable amount of time until eventually I could take no more, and asked May if he would actually share this information with me.

'Oh, right. Yes. Of course. Right. Well, the key to The Stig, as we all know, is speed. But the question is … what is speed? Is it, for example, just distance over time? Is it even a physical concept at all? Is it also, or instead, a philosophical notion, a blend of the actual acceleration of matter, the physical manifestation of speed if you like, with what Immanuel Kant would call the *perception* of speed, something that exists purely in the mind?'

May continued in this vein for a period I was unable to register at the time, but which my digital tape recorder later told me was 57 minutes. I was snapped from my trance by May urgently exclaiming that I was about to allow my biscuit to fall into my tea.

I hastily made an excuse about being completely absorbed by his words and, since my drink was by now rather cold, May offered to put the kettle on again.

'It's nice to meet someone who's not simply obsessed with fatuous superficialities but likes to dig down into a bit of detail,' May shouted from the kitchen area. 'I've said to Clarkson and Hammond many times that we should do a *Top Gear* item on the philosophical roots of speed, but they just tell me to shut up.'

May returned to stand behind the battered sofa opposite and brought proceedings back to The Stig.

'So, as I was saying, he may have incredible reactions, but there's more to it than that. It's not just about how quickly he can apply opposite lock at 150 m.p.h. I believe The Stig goes one further. I believe he actually has pure speed in his very soul.'

May must have sensed my scepticism. 'Trust me, this will all make sense once I explain how he actually came to exist,' he said breezily, as he returned to the kitchen to silence the whistling kettle.

After pouring me another cup of tea, May sat back on the sofa, pressed his fingers together in front of his face and continued: 'The key to The Stig is Concorde,' he began. 'His mother was an air stewardess on Concorde, an extremely attractive young lady and ... well, how can I put this? Erm ... she was a bit of a good-time girl, so to speak. On one of her Concorde flights from New York to London, one of the passengers happened to be a legendary American test pilot. He had taken experimental jets up to Mach 2, 3, and 4 several times, a real hot shot – his catchphrase, I believe, was, "I feel the need ... the need for speed." You can imagine the type. He was also very handsome, very dashing and, during the flight, he and this stewardess sort of made eyes at one another and, you know, no doubt used suggestive words such as "Hullo" and all that, and, erm ... well, one thing led to another and before you knew it, he and this lady were heading for the lavatory cubicle to, you know, sort of ... consummate ... erm ...'

May seemed a little flushed and slightly embarrassed by this tale. He fell silent for a moment and began cleaning the tip of a spark plug with a cotton bud. Eventually, I asked if he would continue.

'Ah, yes, okay. So the stewardess and the test pilot are in the lavatory busy, you know, joining the, erm ... mile high club, as it were. And, well, right at the moment that the gentleman ... how can I put this? Right at the moment that he, erm, you know, emptied the Hoover bag and ... erm ... you know ... umm ... released the Swarfega ... what I mean is, at the moment at which he *went supersonic*, so did Concorde. It passed through the sound barrier at exactly the same second.'

May paused to take a sip of his tea and carefully consume another Rich Tea biscuit before carrying on with his story.

'As I believe often happens with these dalliances, the lady found herself in the family way,' he whispered. 'And, nine months later, a baby boy was born, a baby boy conceived aboard Concorde at the precise moment that the aircraft entered supersonic flight. This unique circumstance meant that speed was fused directly into the child's soul.'

It was a remarkable, if rather odd story, but May wasn't finished yet.

'Now, obviously the girl and the airline top brass don't want a scandal and nor does the test pilot and the US Air Force, so the lady disappears off to a quiet place in the countryside to bring up her son without drawing any attention. The problem is, as soon as he can walk he starts running at incredible speeds and when he gets his first tricycle he pedals it so fast the wheels and pedals all start smoking and burst into flames. His mother and father are terrified that his secret will get out so they do the only thing they can do – they forbid him from showing his speed.'

My heart sank. This sounded almost exactly like the story of the little boy called Dash in the popular Pixar animated film, *The Incredibles*. Fearing I was wasting my time talking to another lunatic, I raised this issue with May.

'What's *The Incredibles*?' he replied, furrowing his brow. 'No, I'm afraid I'm not aware of that. Was it a cinematic release? Oh. Well, I'm afraid I've never seen it. I don't go to the pictures very often. Where was I? Ah, yes, so this young chap is still the living embodiment of speed and no matter how much they try to stop him, he keeps demonstrating his incredible skill at every opportunity. Finally, in desperation, they send him to see a Grand Master of Slowness – my cousin, Stanley May, known to his RAF colleagues as Squadron Leader Slow. More tea?'

May refilled both our mugs, added milk and then stirred each 12 times anti-clockwise, then 12 times clockwise.

'Good old Stanley was known throughout the Air Force for his four-hour pre-flight checks,' May continued. 'He was famous for it. "The war will be over before Stan is in the air" they used to say. So he was the ideal sort of chap to slow this boy down. And I gather he did rather well. He'd slowed him right down, to the point where he could watch a game of cricket or concentrate on an entire edition of *Countryfile* without getting restless. But then, sadly, everything went a bit pear-shaped ...'

What, I wondered, had gone wrong? May sat back on the sofa and crossed one leg across his other knee. He noticed a small smudge on his work boot and began rubbing at it, before leaping to his feet and disappearing into the kitchen, eventually returning with a small shoe-polishing kit that he carefully unpacked, selecting a brush to apply a small amount of black boot polish before picking out a second brush with which he expertly buffed away the residual polish and brought the errant boot back to a perfect shine. He then returned to the kitchen and put away the polishing kit before returning to his seat. As it had been a good ten minutes since he had last spoken, I reminded him where he was up to in his story.

'Ah, yes, it all went wrong and I'm sure you're wondering why. Well, it went wrong because of *Top Gear*. He somehow got wind that the programme was coming back and that they were looking for a racing driver. Well, he was there like a shot and they gave him the job. All he had to do was make sure he never removed his crash helmet or spoke a single word, and his parents would never know that he was brazenly flaunting his exceptional speed abilities on national television. It was the perfect ruse, and no-one would ever know. Clarkson still doesn't, of course; crashing about the place with his stupid super-soldier idea rather than listening to what my cousin told me, which is the truth, I can assure you.'

May leant over the arm of the sofa, picked up an unspecified motorcycle part from the floor and began examining it in minute detail. The silence became mildly uncomfortable and, sensing that our chat was over, I thanked him for his time and said I would be leaving.

'You're very welcome,' May said distractedly, still examining the motorcycle component. 'Would you mind letting yourself out? I've just noticed a small piece of fluff trapped inside the inner housing here, and I really must remove it immediately.'

I walked through the kitchen and into the hallway. As I headed towards the front door I noticed the door to May's study was open and I paused to take a quick look inside. As I did, I could hear a murmuring voice carrying through the kitchen from the workshop beyond: 'Oh, dear, Alan Alternator, you seem to have got yourself into quite a pickle ...' It was May. He appeared to be fully distracted talking to his motorcycle part.

I used his distraction to poke my head fully through the part-open door of his office and was immediately struck by several framed pictures on the wall above a large desk, all of them depicting the supersonic airliner, Concorde. Below these multiple images of the same aeroplane, on the desk itself, was an inkwell, an immaculate blotter and a sturdy Grundig television atop a large VHS player. On a small rack to the back of desk lay a neatly arranged row of video cassettes. I stepped cautiously into the room to read the titles on their spines. There was *Top Gun*, Tom Cruise's iconic portrayal of a fighter jock who falls in love; *The Right Stuff*, the seminal film about test pilots who risked all to go faster than the speed of sound; and *Concorde: The Lovely Ladies Who Served in Her*, a documentary narrated by Raymond Baxter.

All at once I experienced the same sinking feeling of futility that had swept over me upon discovering the DVDs in Clarkson's bag. Quietly, I let myself out of the house, fearing that James May had spent too long on his own in his private garage-cum-workshop.

5

RICHARD HAMMOND ON THE STIG

'Oh, May's definitely spent too long on his own in his private garage-cum-workshop,' Richard Hammond said breezily, when we spoke on the telephone the following day. 'Come down to my place tomorrow and I'll set you straight,' he added, in a tone that gave me great hope.

The long drive to his house on a turbulent Sunday afternoon gave me time to take stock of what I had learned about The Stig from his two colleagues. The answer, sadly, was almost nothing, except that both presenters seemed quite peculiar. I had hoped for fascinating tales about the origins of The Stig, but what I had heard was largely the useless ramblings of two men who appeared lost in a confused world somewhere between fact and movie fiction.

I hoped it would be third time lucky with Hammond. Of the trio, he was the youngest, the most up-to-date, the chirpiest and the least cynical.

As I drove deeper into the countryside, the A-roads became B-roads and then gave way to winding, narrow lanes. Hammond had warned me that his house was quite hard to find and he was right. When my increasingly befuddled sat-nav began to believe we were driving across a lake, I admitted defeat and stopped to ask for directions at a rambling old pub called The Gutted Ferret.

Some bunting left over from the Queen's Jubilee celebrations was still hanging over the bar, a reminder of how good she'd looked in 1977. From behind the bar, the barman stared at me with his one eye. Unnerved, I looked at the two customers at the bar. Both of them returned my gaze with their single working eyes. I told them I was looking for Richard Hammond's house.

'Mester 'Ammond? Eh, laaaast I saw 'im was in 'ere on Ladies' Noiyt,' said the barman. 'That be the noiyt we let ladies come in 'ere. Seth don't loike thaaat at all, does thar, Seth?'

The chap to my right grunted. 'Arr hep nar toimes an barr willont roight,' he said.

'Oi once sarr a goiant metal bird up in the skoy,' added the third chap, before returning to staring at the pint of cloudy, pale orange liquid in front of him.

Armed with some moderately confusing directions, I left the pub and eventually pulled into the long, narrow track that led to Richard Hammond's house. As I climbed from the car, I noticed across the lawn a circle of rune stones arranged around a stone slab decorated with stars and circles drawn in dried blood, and what appeared to be the remains of a sacrificed goat.

'Welcome, welcome,' shouted Hammond, bounding from the front door. He noticed me still staring at the curious arrangement on his lawn. 'Ah, yes, sorry about that. We had a bit of a barbecue last night and I haven't cleared up yet. Don't worry about the symbols, it's just a local party game – sort of like *Pictionary* mixed with *Twister*.'

At that moment there was a howling cry from some nearby bushes and a man brandishing a pitchfork burst from within. He stopped a few feet away, his one good eye blazing with anger: 'Thar be a witch! Aaarh! Get thee gone, witch! Burn thee!' he shouted, and raised his pitchfork as if to stab me.

'No, Mungo! Down!' snapped Hammond and, to my relief, the man stepped back.

'You'll have to excuse him. He's saying these things because ... erm ... he's just read a *Which?* magazine article about ... pitchforks. Yes, pitchforks. Quite upsetting for him, because his model scored very badly for reliability. Go on, off you go, Mungo. This man isn't from *Which?* magazine.'

The bumpkin slunk off back into the bushes muttering to himself, and Hammond led me into the house, past a row of monks' habits hung on pegs in the hallway. 'Costumes for the school play,' he said quickly, as we continued into the kitchen. My host gestured for me to take my place at a large oak table in the centre of the room.

I began to explain that I was still looking for information about the origins of The Stig but that Clarkson and May had not been as helpful as I had hoped.

'Let me guess.' Hammond sighed as he sat down opposite me. 'One told you he's a super-soldier created by the American military and the other said he was the product of a supersonic shag on Concorde. Yeah. I've heard those stories a hundred times. I'm afraid they're complete drivel. You have to understand that Jeremy thinks Tom Clancy novels are non-fiction and May is so senile he's constantly getting told off for accidentally landing his light aeroplane on the M4. They're basically idiots.' He leaned back in his chair and laughed. 'The worrying thing is,' he continued, 'they really believe their own theories. It's just a shame they're … you know … a load of old bollocks.'

At that moment we were interrupted by the arrival of an old woman, clearly some sort of housekeeper. ''Scuse me, Mester 'Ammond, but them vestal virgins has arroived,' she croaked, fixing me with a suspicious glare from her single functioning eye.

'Ah! Erm … good!' Hammond shouted, rather too loudly. 'Virgin has got back to you about those flights, then? Thank you, old widow woman. But I've realised I don't want them at the moment so please could you … erm … tell the *flights* to *go away*.'

The old woman muttered under her breath and shuffled out of the room.

Hammond looked slightly wide-eyed for a moment and then regained his composure.

'Sorry, where were we?' he said, quietly. 'Oh, yes, The Stig. I'm sorry you had to put up with Clarkson and May and their drivel. If you want to know about The Stig I can fill you in, though I warn you that the truth isn't as fantastical and interesting as the stuff they've told you.'

I told him that all I wanted was the truth, and invited him to continue.

'Well, I do know the truth about his origins.' He smiled, fiddling with his cuff. 'And the reason I know the truth is that his roots are right here, in the countryside. It's a story that's been told around campfires and in village halls, and passed down from father to son for generations.'

Hammond paused for effect, his gelled hair silhouetted against the gathering storm clouds visible through the window behind him.

'Many years ago – nobody knows quite when – a boy was born. Sadly, his mother died in childbirth and the father, who was a racehorse trainer, was left to bring up the young lad by himself. Now the main problem was, the father was a proud man and he wouldn't ask for help, so he has no choice but to take the baby to work with him. But then once he's there, he can't just leave the baby sitting in the stables whilst he's out riding the horses, so he came up with a clever solution. He fashioned a sort of papoose arrangement so that he could carry the baby on his chest and, since there were no riding hats in baby size, he fashioned one from a white bowl. I should add at this point that since his wife died, the baby is the only thing in his life and he calls it his little angel, which is why he also always dresses it entirely in white. Anyway, the next crucial thing is, when the father put the baby in the papoose he strapped him in facing forward. And he noticed that the faster the horse went, the more excited the baby became. At full gallop he was screaming with joy, and whenever they slowed down the little chap would start howling in frustration. Now, clearly this means that the first real sensation the child ever experienced was speed, and speed in its purest, rawest form, on a horse at full gallop. The neural paths in his brain were being fused together at this vital stage of development, and speed was the primary experience. Plus, the kid is with his daddy, so the whole experience is reassuring and fun. Wrap all that together, and you can understand how speed would become the driving force in his life. Do you see what I mean?'

I said that I did. Outside, there was a distant clap of thunder and fat drops of rain began to streak against the window.

Hammond glanced at the worsening weather. 'Oh, dear, someone's angered Ambisagrus the rain god,' he muttered, under his breath.

'Anyway,' he said, quickly. 'One day, the father found a beautifully long stretch of flat, open ground that went on forever. The stables had just bought this incredible racehorse, which they hoped would be the fastest flat racer ever, and the father thought this would be the perfect place to take the new horse to top speed. So, with the baby strapped to his chest, they set off and, sure enough, the horse was faster than anything they'd ever ridden. It was blasting across the ground as if in mid air, the little baby screaming with pleasure. But, they were going so fast that they didn't see a particular patch of ground in front of them until it was too late. The ground was covered in symbols drawn in chalk, and when the horse went over them, they were completely destroyed. They stopped to see what it was they'd gone over and, at that moment, a man dressed like a wizard with a white beard, wearing a pointy hat and carrying a wand came rushing towards them. He was so angry his sacred ground had been defiled that he waved his wand and put a spell on the father and baby. "Expeliamus! Cockus Knobus! You shall henceforth never be able to enjoy the thing that thou enjoyest the most, whatever that may be!" he shouted, and then he disappeared.'

Hammond paused. From somewhere outside a distant chanting could be heard. 'Bloody Scouts having a sing-song,' he said, briskly. 'So, the little baby grows into a man and, cursed by the spell, he spends his life going faster and faster, trying in vain to feel once more that pleasure he used to get from the thrill of speed, still dressed all in white; only now he's got a job that allows him the maximum time to chase the elusive thrill of speed, which is driving round and round the *Top Gear* test track. That's right!' the diminutive presenter concluded triumphantly. 'He's The Stig!'

If nothing else, Hammond's story seemed rather more plausible than those told by Clarkson and May. I thanked him for being so honest with me.

'It's my pleasure,' he said, with a smile. 'Listen, it's really coming down out there now and these lanes can get pretty treacherous. You're very welcome to stay the night.'

It was a very kind offer and one I happily accepted.

'Good,' he said, beckoning me into the sitting room next door. 'Tell you what, I'll get the old crone to bring us some broth and we can stick on a DVD or something.'

I said that sounded very agreeable as a one-eyed black cat shot from under an armchair in the corner.

'Right then,' Hammond said cheerily. 'Any preferences? I've got all the Harry Potter films or we could watch my absolutely favourite, *Seabiscuit* ...'

Suddenly I felt quite sick, hurriedly made my excuses and took my chances driving back to civilisation through the stormy and probably entirely wasted evening.

6

'WHO IS THE STIG?'

My conversations with the three *Top Gear* presenters had not been as fruitful as I had hoped. I resolved not to be too crestfallen about their frankly idiotic theories and instead take my search for the truth about The Stig back to basics. It seemed that the TG trio knew little of use about The Stig, but what about the wider world?

At the start of this book I noted that a question about The Stig is one of the most widely searched terms on the whole of the internet, and I realised that I had yet to attempt this online search for myself. I must admit I have mixed feelings about internet searches after paying the heavy legal price for foolishly committing to print a 'fact' I had found on the web without verifying the source. Once again, I can only state in the clearest possible terms that Dannii Minogue does NOT have a penis.

I decided, however, to make use of a search engine whilst on a train to Manchester for a meeting about my forthcoming Jeremy Kyle biography, *Ringleader of Idiots.* My journey was delayed by a defective passenger at Stafford and I decided to use my time wisely by opening the web browser on my smart phone and typing in that ever-popular question: 'Who is The Stig?'

Unsurprisingly, my search returned hundreds of thousands of results. Some of them were out-dated, some of them were deceptive, some of them were a gateway to a very strong kind of pornography. There were, however, many more links that gave interesting insights into the web's view of the man behind the visor.

I started by following a link to gearboxers.net, a popular online forum for car enthusiasts.

The thread started with a simple question from a contributor calling themselves 'AwesomePunto1981': 'Does anyone know who The Stig is?'

Almost immediately, this attracted a blunt reply from a user called 'MiataHead' which said, 'No-one knows. That's the point, idiot.'

Others were more sympathetic to the question: 'It was Alain Prost. Now they just stick a homeless man in the suit and fake all the laps,' said 'StuGH1990'.

'Everyone knows it's Damon Hill,' countered 'Ferrari328GTS', whilst a user called 'MaserNut Steve' added, 'Damon stopped doing it years ago. It's usually Lewis Hamilton unless he's busy, then Paul di Resta does it.'

The thread continued in this vein of unsubstantiated opinions communicated with baseless confidence until the general brevity of writing was broken by a contributor who left a lengthy and remarkably well-written theory about 'super-soldiers' and a 'top secret US military project'. I read to the bottom of this strangely familiar tale before all too late checking the contributor's name, which was listed as 'Cleremy Jarkson'.

Moving swiftly on, I looked in on some more forums and message boards and found more of the same noisy but baseless opinion presented as fact then rapidly getting sidetracked into name-calling or an irrelevant debate about whether Jessica Ennis was 'fit'. The main conclusions I drew from my rail-bound browsing were that The Stig provokes a lot of debate and that the internet was full of idiots.

Nonetheless, when I returned home that evening I went online and sought out a popular chatroom site in order to canvas some real-time views on The Stig's identity, signing up as user 'SDBM' and entering the 'general chat' arena. The conversation went as follows:

SDBM> Who is The Stig?

CraterDude> Like off Topgear???

SDBM> Yes, The Stig off *Top Gear*.

CraterDude> Why do you ask?????

MaximumMax> It's Nigel Mansell.

CraterDude> What does your user name mean?

LooneeGurl> I heart top gear!!!!!11111!!!!!

CraterDude> Is it what I think it is?????

LooneeGurl> Richard Hamond is amaaaaaaaaaaze!!!!!!!11!!!!1 LOL

CraterDude> We can't talk about SDBM in here. Do you know how to find the special interest chatroom?

LooneeGurl> I HEART Richard and Jemrey and James!!!!! 11111!! TG ROOLZ!!!!!1111!!!

SDBM> My user name is simply based on my real name.

MaximumMax> Yeah right. Dirty sod.

CraterDude> It's okay SDBM, you're amongst friends.

SDBM> I really just wondered if anyone had any views on who The Stig is.

CraterDude> I understand ;) Are you new to the scene?????

MaximumMax> This is GENERAL chat FFS.

CraterDude> What are you wearing????

MaximumMax> Stop this.

CraterDude> Do you like leather????

MaximumMax> If this doesn't stop I will report you to a moderator.

CraterDude> Are you a big man SDBM?????

NotHammond> The Stig is the son of a well-known horse trainer who used to strap him to his front when riding these thoroughbred horses, giving him the very purest and rawest sense of speed from a young age. Unfortunately, he was then hit with a wizard's curse and would be forced to spend the rest of his days vainly seeking the thrill he once got from those youthful horseback rides with his father.

>>>> SDBM has left the conversation

LooneeGurl> THE STIIIIIG YEEEEAH!!!!!111!!!

My chatroom experiment had not been a great success. However, I was still keen to know what the man (or woman) in the street thought of The Stig and, a couple of days later, with 45 minutes to kill in central London before an unrelated meeting with Carol Thatcher, I decided to find this out in the most literal way possible. I positioned myself on a moderately busy thoroughfare and began stopping people at random to ask them, very simply, who they thought The Stig was.

'Sorry, I'm in a hurry' and 'Sod off' seemed to be popular responses, but I did get a few more articulate answers during my time on the pavement.

'You know that German bird they had on *Top Gear*?' said a man called Neil, in painty overalls. 'Helga or Seltzer or something? Well, it's her. They tape down her knockers and pretend she's a bloke. That's why she can't speak. Everyone would realise she's German. And a bird.'

An enlightening view, but one that was not shared by a gentleman identifying himself as 'Yaz', who took a rather different approach: 'Stig is like this robot dude who got kidnapped by aliens?' he said, with a pointlessly questioning intonation. 'And then he was pumped for information about earth, yeah, and then in return, yeah, they let him come back down to earth, yeah, and they'd given him super-skills, yeah, and the super-skill he uses most is driving, yeah, and that's why he's The Stig? Either that, or it's Michael Schumacher?'

A casually dressed Cockney gentleman called Steve was more confident in his opinions.

'I hear this a lot: "Who's The Stig, mate?" Who's The Stig?' he said, holding up one hand and making a strange mouth movement as if working a puppet. 'Well, I'll tell you who The Stig is, mate. My brother, right, he met this geezer down a pub in East Ham, right, and this geezer, he was best mates with this bloke, right, who knew a geezer whose cousin worked at, like, a Formula 1 team like McLaren or McWilliams or one of them, right, and he said this geezer's cousin had told this geezer that everyone, right, in F1, right, knew who it was but that it was, like, a total secret and that if anyone in F1 ever told, right, they'd get the sack, right, or, like, demoted down to, like, F5 or summat, so no-one ever said nothing, right, but this geezer or his cousin or whoever, he don't work for the team no more so he was, like, ready to, like, spill the beans and all that.'

The Cockney man seemed very confident in his story and I asked him to continue to its natural, revelatory conclusion: who was The Stig?

'Well, that's the thing, mate,' the Cockney man said. 'Can't remember. Maybe John something? Or Dave? Alan? I dunno, mate. Sorry.' And with that he strolled away.

Shortly afterwards, a group of young Japanese girls told me The Stig was 'super amazing One Direction' (although they may have misunderstood the question), whilst an unusually dressed lady with a heavily pierced head rather aggressively labelled him and the other *Top Gear* presenters as 'fascist pigs'.

Finally, a hunched and grey-haired old lady approached me and declared that she had a theory about The Stig. 'I hope you don't mind me butting in,' she said politely, in a quavering, slightly Bristolian accent. 'I'm rather a fan of the television broadcast you're referring to and I just wanted to tell you a theory I have about the origins of that Stig chap. Are you familiar with the supersonic aircraft, Concorde ...?'

I'm ashamed to say that at this moment I snapped and barked, 'For God's sake, I've heard your theory already!' at the crudely disguised James May whilst pushing him away from me and causing him to topple to the ground.

Shocked by my own strength, I guiltily helped the fallen presenter to his feet and realised that it was not James May in a headscarf and raincoat: it really was a rather sweet old lady and she really did have a theory about The Stig.

I apologised profusely and explained that I had mistaken her for James May, which she very graciously said 'happened all the time', before explaining her theory to me and to the two police officers who had been summoned by a passer-by.

'My late husband was an aeronautical engineer,' she said, carefully, 'and so I picked up a few bits and pieces of knowledge from that sphere over the years. One of the things I remember is that commercial aeroplanes are very often white. As you may know, white objects reflect heat and that helps to prevent the aircraft cabin from heating up at altitude. Concorde is a marvellous example of that, a wonderful machine, although of course she used to get rather hot inside I'm told, and of course she expanded greatly in supersonic flight. It's the friction as well, you see.'

The old lady really did seem to know a remarkable amount about aeronautical technology. 'Now I watch a lot of *Top Gear* with my grandchildren,' she continued. 'And something I noticed about The Stig is that he wears a white suit. But in the old days, it was black. Of course, the Lockheed SR-71 was a supersonic aircraft that was very, very dark blue rather than white, hence it was called the "Blackbird" because it actually looked black, and it got its colour from the heat-resistant paint that covered its fuselage, which was deliberate, since it encouraged heat to radiate from the aircraft whilst also making it harder to see. So it seems to me that both white and black can have advantages in aircraft construction and I wondered if they had any advantages where The Stig was concerned – perhaps related to dissipation of heat under the extreme conditions of driving at high speed for long periods of time and being unable to remove the suit and the crash helmet for reasons of anonymity.'

The policemen and I were fascinated to know more. What was the well-informed old lady's conclusions about this colour variance in The Stig?

'Well, I have thought about this quite a lot,' she said, slowly. 'And I can't think of anything. It's all a load of bollocks. Sorry, my dear. I think The Stig is probably Jenson Button. Ta-ra!'

The old lady had been remarkably knowledgeable about aircraft and remarkably disappointing in her conclusion. As I established that no charges would be pressed and called it a day, I realised my attempt to ask the world 'Who is The Stig?' had left me with two conclusions: firstly, there were many theories but no clear consensus. And, secondly, pushing a pensioner to the ground in central London will make you late for a meeting with Carol Thatcher.

However, the old lady's ultimately pointless theorising had raised an issue about The Stig that I knew I needed to address sooner rather than later: his apparent change in colour.

7

THE BLACK STIG

When *Top Gear* returned to our screens in 2002, The Stig was black and remained so until the beginning of the third series when he was apparently 'killed off' in an unfortunate accident on an aircraft carrier, after which a white Stig took over. It has long been accepted that these were two different Stigs, yet this fact was immediately dispelled when, in the course of my early research, I met with former *Top Gear* associate producer, Ridley Smeen, in a quiet edit suite.

'Trust me, it was the same Stig,' he said, firmly, smacking a pen against the side of the edit desk for emphasis. 'He just changed colour, and we had to think of something to get round it.'

Like the old Jaguar XJS that supposedly killed black Stig, Smeen's story certainly holds a surprising amount of water. There is plenty of evidence from before *Top Gear*'s return to suggest that The Stig was as white as he is today: in particular, a remarkable photograph that came to light after I performed a motorsport-related search in the archives of Surrey local newspaper, *The Guildford Trombone*. There, under the headline, 'GROWN UP SPOILS KARTING DAY' was a picture of a man in a distinctive white racing suit and crash helmet, standing on the top step of a small podium holding a small trophy. Two disappointed-looking children occupied the second and third place steps either side of him and a banner in the background read, 'Happy 12th birthday Craig!' The short and remarkably uninformative story underneath the photo told me it was taken at the Come! Go! karting track in Guildford. I called the number on their website and the owner, Steve Hampson, seemed keen for me to come down and speak to him.

'In the early 2000s, not long after we'd opened, this chap in a white suit used to show up, already in his helmet, take out one of the karts and just smash the lap record again and again,' Hampson recalls when we met at his facility one fine evening in March. 'Never said a word, just drove. I always thought it was Ayrton Senna in disguise but, you know, not dead.'

For over a year, Hampson saw the mysterious white-suited figure at least once a week, often more, until a fateful day in early 2002 when the track owner noticed something unusual: 'It was Friday the 22nd of February. I'll always remember that because it was also the day I had my letter read out on Radio 2's *Steve Wright In The Afternoon*. Around four o'clock this fella walks in, suit on, crash helmet on – it looks like our usual regular, but he's all in black. I didn't really think too much of it, I just thought he was going for a new look or something. But then he gets out on the track and he's a good second or so down on his usual lap times. There was definitely something up. It was almost like he was a bit down in the dumps. I mean, what with the black and everything, it was like he was in mourning. It was all really weird. I should have been more worried I suppose, but I was just totally buzzing from having Wrighty read my letter out. And also because at the time I was addicted to really strong painkillers.'

What could have happened to cause this change in The Stig's demeanour and appearance? Did the shift in colour hint at some significant event in the life of The Stig himself – something so earth-shattering that it could trigger such a fundamental shift?

Without the ability to ask the man himself, I started to think laterally. Was it in some way related to the precise date that Steve Hampson was so clearly able to remember? I started my search in the most logical place, looking for anything motorsport-related that may have upset or annoyed The Stig in some way. Sadly, a comprehensive trawl of every major motor-racing publication archive in the country yielded nothing of significance on or around that date.

I broadened my search to a wider newspaper archive and almost immediately hit upon a story from the world of show business that seemed somehow to ring out from all the other news around it: Friday 22 February 2002 was the day that news broke about the sad death of the actor, John Thaw. Could it be that The Stig was in mourning for him? It seemed strange but, as ever with biography writing, one cannot dismiss a lead until it has been proven to be impossible, illegal or likely to make Delia Smith angry again. I needed to get to the bottom of this possible link, and I was going to do it by speaking to the one person in my contacts book who might be able shed more light on it: Dennis Waterman.

Waterman agreed to meet me in a café adjoining the leather jacket shop near Esher, and immediately gave credence to my theory about The Stig's sudden change of colour. 'John did have a mate called Stig, way back when,' the veteran actor said over a cup of coffee and a book of lining samples. 'He was this geezer who did a load of our driving stunts on *The Sweeney.* Funny bloke he was, always had the white lid on, didn't say much; but I tell you what, he could chuck a Ford Granada 3.0 Ghia around the place like no-one else I've ever seen. Never did know his proper name, we just used to call him Stig.'

Waterman confirmed that during filming on the classic 1970s cop show, Thaw and 'Stig' the stunt driver formed a lasting friendship. 'Him and John, they was always standing around on set together, doing the *Daily Express* quick crossword or something like that,' the *Minder* star remembered. 'I dunno what happened to this bloke after we finished doing *Sweeney*, but I do know John kept in touch with him,' he continued, carefully sipping around the ruched foam on his cappuccino. 'Yeah, good mates they were. I never got a bloody word out of the geezer, but him and John, they were thick as thieves.'

Waterman's recollections were fascinating, but I was still puzzled as to how The Stig (or at least someone very like him) had got a job on a gritty 1970s TV police drama. To find out, I contacted producer Nigel Rochelle-Silk, who worked on all four series of *The Sweeney*, and he agreed to speak to me on the phone from his home in Weybridge.

'Oh, *The Sweeney*, love. Those were great days,' the ITV stalwart reminisced. 'Dear old Johnny Thaw and lovely Denny Waterman, we had such a fun time. Such a hoot, it was. Very gritty, of course. After a day's filming, I usually needed a shower, just because of all the grit. Oh, gosh, yes. And the budgets! Not like nowadays, oh, no – we had proper money back then. You remember the classic line, "You're nicked, sunshine!"? Eight writers that took. We had the money to do it properly, you see. I'd say to the accountant, "Mr Waterman will need a new leather jacket for this episode", and he'd give me a million pounds to have one made, just like that. These days they'd use an off-the-peg jacket, or put the jacket in later using CGI. It's just not the same.'

I steered Rochelle-Silk onto the matter of a mysterious stunt driver known as 'Stig', and wondered how he came to work on the programme.

'Well, we had stunt drivers coming out of our ears, love,' the producer recalls. 'But I do remember that chap. Never sure where he came from but I do know that if the director said, "I want this Ford Cortina to drive through that puddle at precisely so-and-so angle", he was the only man for the job. You know the whole thing with driving through the cardboard boxes? Well, that was him who came up with it. Everyone always credits *Starsky and Hutch*, the American brutes, but it was Stig on our lovely *Sweeney* who invented it. It was all a bit of an accident, you see. The boxes were there just as set dressing and Stig was supposed to skid around them. But, just before the take, I remember dear old Johnny Thaw told Stig that the boxes contained a load of David Essex records. What a joker he was, dear, dear, Johnny. Well, Stig hated David Essex you see, so when the director called 'Action!' he really went for it and deliberately smashed through all the boxes! They were empty, of course, but the shot looked fabulous! We were all cheering, the director was over the moon; it was just wonderful! Well, after that we kept telling Stig the boxes contained things he hated. Space Hoppers, cream soda, Frank Bough and so on. He'd hit them every time! Oh, wonderful days!'

By now in the full flow of reminiscence, Rochelle-Silk told me that the only problem with using 'Stig' as the star stunt driver was his choice of dress: 'Of course, there was a bit of a kerfuffle with his crash helmet,' the producer recalled. 'Bright white it was, and he refused to take it off. Absolutely refused. Well, it would have shown up on camera like that so the make-up department, God love 'em, they gave it the full makeover – lovely flesh tones, a toupee on top ... Looking at it on telly, you'd never know it wasn't someone's head. Then at the end of the shoot, it'd just wash off again and he'd be off to the pub with dear old Johnny Thaw. Very good friends, they were. But that was Johnny for you. He'd talk to anyone. Even someone who didn't talk back.'

Whether *The Sweeney* stunt driver 'Stig' and The Stig are one and the same, it is hard to tell, but it seems certain that our modern-day Stig was affected profoundly by the death of the man who used to be Inspector Morse. In February 2002, he turned black as a mark of respect and just eight months later, still in his mourning colour, he made his debut on *Top Gear*.

What seems odd is that The Stig remained black until some time in late summer 2003 when, seemingly without reason, he turned white again. Only The Stig himself can know for sure why he felt he had mourned enough, but analysis of the TV schedules from the period shows that around then, satellite channel *UK Shooters & Boobs* started showing repeats of *The Sweeney*, and perhaps this was nostalgic impetus enough for The Stig to move on with his life.

For the *Top Gear* team, however, The Stig's change of colour was an unforeseen headache, as former associate producer Ridley Smeen explained to me: 'We were ready to shoot some items at the track for series three so I summoned The Stig using Method K, with the scissor lift and the dolphin parts,' Smeen recalled. 'When he appeared, he was a different bloody colour! I couldn't believe it. A few of us tried to have a word with him but he just did that thing where he walks off while you're still speaking.'

In the end, the production team came up with a cunning plan to cover The Stig's sudden colour change. 'We couldn't try to explain it on air,' Smeen confessed, leaning back in his edit suite chair and twirling a Biro between his fingers. 'Apart from anything else, how could we? We didn't know what was going on ourselves. We were busy hoping he didn't suddenly go bright yellow halfway through a shoot or something. So we decided we'd appear to kill off black Stig and then "introduce" white Stig as a new character. We had a replica black suit made up, set up this speed attempt on HMS *Invincible* and nobody was any the wiser. Everyone assumed poor old black Stig had drowned when, the truth is, no-one really died out at sea. Apart from one of the cameramen, but that wasn't our fault. It was a matter for the Shark Police to sort out, if they exist. Which, as it turns out, they don't.'

Top Gear had successfully covered up The Stig's strange change of colour. Whilst we might never know if he was the same 'Stig' that performed driving stunts for *The Sweeney*, in the absence of any better explanation, there is something touching in the possibility that his infamous 'black phase' was a mark of respect for a much-loved former colleague. Did this move speak of a well-concealed tenderness within The Stig's cool exterior? It was hard to know what was going on inside his head, but for my next piece of research I vowed to get as close to being The Stig himself as I possibly could.

8

BEING THE STIG

It seems obvious that The Stig enjoys a unique world view. Not just with his musical and culinary tastes (of which, more to come later) and his rather unconventional social skills; but also quite literally, as he remains encased in a crash helmet and is unable (or unwilling) to speak. This must give a person a different take on life and one that I was keen to experience for myself, in line with one of my favourite maxims: 'To *know* a person you must try to *be* that person.' I attempted something similar whilst working on my biography of Keith Richards, *Smack In The Face*, and the results were illuminating, if also life threatening.

So it was that I arranged to hire a white racing suit and a white crash helmet so that I might affect an appearance broadly similar to that of The Stig, and spend a day seeing the world as he would see it.

My day began with a trip to the shops. I had uncovered no evidence thus far that The Stig goes to the shops, but I was sure he must occasionally need, as I did, to buy some hand soap and a printer cartridge. For want of anywhere better, I drove my rented car to Woking and parked in the multi-storey adjacent to the town's large shopping centre.

Almost as soon as I stepped from the car a man walking from his own vehicle gave me a cheery thumbs up and shouted 'Oi-oi, Stiggy!' It was a remarkable unsolicited reaction and would prove to be the first of many.

Negotiating my way to the shops themselves, I soon discovered that my earnest attempts to find the places I needed were almost totally derailed by a constant stream of attention from people videoing me on their mobile phones, shouting 'STIG!' at high volume in close proximity to me, or physically accosting me and demanding to photograph their friend Dazza with his arm around me. Is this how The Stig has to lead his life? Is even the simplest trip to Boots a never-ending ordeal of attention?

Eventually, the ever-expanding and excitable mob seething around me became too much and, as I posed with what seemed like a sea of over 50 children, I did what I suspect The Stig himself never would. I spoke.

'I'm not the real Stig!' I blurted out, and then repeated it for good measure.

The effect was rather more dramatic than I had anticipated. The visible disappointment amongst the children was matched only by the palpable anger and, in one case, simmering aggression of their parents.

As I left the shopping centre, I felt I had experienced a small part of The Stig's off-camera life, though I had also compromised the experience through blowing my own cover. I felt it unlikely that The Stig himself would ever speak, much less deny it was him; nor would he be asked to leave the premises by security and be called a 'kiddy fiddler' by two complete strangers. I can't say if he would have been able to buy hand soap and ink for his printer. I wasn't.

I returned to my rented car and set off to complete my experience as The Stig by attending his workplace, the *Top Gear* airfield. Racing drivers must get used to operating a vehicle whilst wearing a crash helmet but for those of us not familiar with such a hefty and restrictive piece of headgear, I can report that it restricts both vision and hearing to a troubling degree. Perhaps The Stig doesn't find this a problem. Perhaps he wouldn't have failed to notice that a pedestrian-crossing light was on red, wouldn't have driven through it and wouldn't have found himself in conversation with a police officer whose opening gambit was, 'Is this some sort of joke?'

Once again I was forced to 'break character' and do some very 'un-Stig-like' things such as speaking, removing my crash helmet and going to the boot of the car to retrieve the briefcase which contained my driving licence and rental documents.

I drove the rest of the way across Surrey with the crash helmet off, pausing to put it on again only when I was on the lane leading directly to the main gate of the *Top Gear* aerodrome. Approaching the security hut at the end of the road, the guard stepped forwards to approach my car, narrowed his eyes slightly and then gave a cheery wave and let me drive on without hindrance. It made me feel quite important. I wondered if it has the same effect on The Stig. From what I knew so far, I suspected that he didn't care. I also suspected that he was unlikely to arrive at work in a rented Hyundai.

This was exactly two weeks after my first visit to the *Top Gear* studio and the team was there to record the final show of the current series. I drove down to the production offices, parked the car and stood beside it to see what reaction I would garner. A few people walked past and a couple of them gave me a cheery, 'Hello, Stig' or 'Stiggy!' It occurred to me that they seemed largely pleased to see me, yet also spoke to me as if they had just encountered a familiar and friendly dog. Would this have any effect on The Stig's mental state? I must admit, it wasn't unpleasant to be greeted in this way, and I would have happily tolerated an affectionate pat on the head to go with it. I'm not sure the same could be said of The Stig himself.

It was just after noon. Based on my previous visit, I guessed the presenters would be in the studio rehearsing the day's show, and I decided to pay them a visit.

Jeremy was the first to spot me. 'Stiggy!' he exclaimed, then paused and squinted at me. '*Not* Stiggy!' he corrected himself. I felt it only polite to tell him who I really was. As someone extremely familiar with The Stig, Clarkson quickly dissected my attempts to mimic him.

'Right, so, wrong suit, wrong helmet, wrong walk, and you're speaking, which is wrong,' he said, briskly.

Richard Hammond had joined us. 'And you're carrying a briefcase,' he added, helpfully. 'I've never seen the real Stig do that. I mean, he could, but it's pretty unlikely.'

'Otherwise,' finished Clarkson in a dry tone, 'spot on.'

I put the briefcase back in the car and walked into the production offices. A younger member of the team gave me the same cheery greeting I had heard earlier. The more experienced staff seemed to see through my ruse almost immediately. I was not The Stig.

I sat down on a violently floral sofa in an anteroom just outside The Stig's quarters. Last I had seen, the man himself was rapidly lapping a car on the track outside. I was becoming used to the crash helmet now; there was even something comforting about it, and I kept it on as I began to make notes on my experiences thus far. It really was strangely pleasant to be sealed inside your own little world, safe in the knowledge that people couldn't see your face or second-guess your thoughts. Was this why The Stig was prone to unusual and seemingly rude acts, such as walking off when he was being spoken to? Maybe he had the confidence to do such things because he was safe inside the protective bubble of his crash helmet. I was just making a note of this theory when I was distracted by what sounded like a rapidly approaching fast humming sound. That was the last thing I remember.

When I came round I was lying on the same floral sofa, with two members of the *Top Gear* production team looking down at me.

'We're so sorry,' one of them said. 'We didn't realise he'd react like that.' She handed me an ice pack wrapped in a tea towel, which I pressed to the tender bruises on my arms and chest. It was immediately clear what had happened here: I had been attacked by The Stig himself. I looked down at my fake Stig racing suit. It was torn in several places, and covered in a curious green substance that managed to be both dusty and sticky.

Spending a few hours attempting to be The Stig had been most illuminating. I learned that he is a bona fide celebrity, that he seems largely beloved by those who work with him, and that he is surprisingly hard to mimic with utter conviction.

Most of all, however, I learned that he does not like to be impersonated. Was he aware of his own iconic status, perhaps? Or did he mistake me for another creature of the same type and saw me as a rival? I might never know. The only certain thing was the amount of pain I was in.

It was time to dispense with the fake outfit and attempt to get inside The Stig's head in another way.

9

SPEED DEMON

The tiny yellow Lotus sports car rocketed down the straight towards the next corner. Behind me, its engine roared with powerful exertion whilst above me the air of this once quiet summer day sped over the windscreen and plunged through the gap where the roof would normally be, licking violently around my face, which was bracketed by a crash helmet.

We approached a sizeable and sharply angled corner at a speed that would normally land you in prison and/or a field yet here, on this track, we did not crash. The driver smoothly and calmly applied a significant amount of braking and delicately twisted the steering wheel to feed us briskly into the bend, accompanied by a high-pitched howl from the tyres and an odd sensation of extreme G-force. I can't deny that, to me, the passenger, this was moderately amusing. I also can't deny that it was making me feel rather queasy.

It seemed fair to say that The Stig is defined by speed. It is his friend, his lover; you might even say it is his very reason to be.

Yet, as I had realised this, I had also realised that I had no real sense of what true speed felt like. Certainly, I had been on fast trains and intercontinental aeroplanes, but these give you no real sense of the actual speeds they achieve. I had unexpected experience of raw, naked speed whilst working on my acclaimed Cliff Richard biography, *Young One, Old Neck*, after I fell from a two-storey-high balcony following an altercation with Una Stubbs, but it was brief and ended mercifully in a well-placed swimming pool.

The speed of The Stig's world, the kind of brutal pace that comes only from a highly tuned vehicle unleashed on track, that was something unfamiliar to me and I had resolved to remedy this. I had already dressed up as The Stig (with mixed results, and a rather odd smell on my hands that I couldn't shift); now I needed to feel the velocities and G-force that were The Stig's everyday companions. I hoped that doing so might help me to understand more about the man himself.

So it was that I found myself at the Fenton Ridge race track in the capable hands of Ally McLeish, an instructor from the TrakAttak circuit driving school. McLeish promised to 'take it easy' to start with, but it soon became clear that his idea of 'take it easy' was wildly out of kilter with mine. Listening back to the sound files on my digital tape recorder, I note that on those first three laps I swore 17 times and was sick twice. After that, familiarity gave me less cause to swear, there wasn't anything left to come up and the entire experience became moderately enjoyable, up until the point when McLeish pulled into the pits and told me it was my turn.

To someone used only to driving a normal car on the public highway, piloting a sporty machine like a Lotus Elise around a race track is an alien experience. McLeish encouraged me to rev the engine until long past the point when I would normally change up a gear and to use the brakes later and harder than I would ever consider on the road.

It occurred to me that McLeish was giving me almost constant instruction on my early laps: barking orders about my use of the car, providing detailed information about the way to approach and dispatch each corner, and intermittently reminding me to stop screaming, 'AAARGHHH.' How strange, I thought, that The Stig seems capable of coaching *Top Gear*'s celebrity guests, yet reportedly barely speaks to them at all. Could he really communicate all the complex and unfamiliar information necessary to facilitate competent track driving using only gestures, or was there some deeper force at work here? Is The Stig blessed with psychic powers?

Whilst on a break from track driving at Fenton Ridge, I received a telephone call from Richard Hammond asking if I had found out any more about 'horses and wizard stuff'. I mumbled that it was 'slow going' and distracted him from further questioning by taking the opportunity to ask if it was possible that The Stig possessed the ability to transfer his thoughts to other people?

'What an odd question,' the presenter started. 'But, now you mention it, there was this time when The Stig came into the room and I immediately started thinking about a corned beef sandwich. Mind you, it was lunch time. And I do like corned beef. So that was probably a coincidence.'

Did Hammond have any other experiences that might lead him to think The Stig was capable of complex mind-control tricks?

'Oh my God, I've just remembered something else,' the *Top Gear* star suddenly exclaimed at the other end of the line. 'The desk we use to write the studio scripts for the show. It used to face one way and then suddenly, without warning, we came in one day and it was facing in the opposite direction. Maybe The Stig had moved it ... *with his mind.* Although, on reflection, I do remember Jeremy saying, "Can someone turn that desk around when they've got a minute – it would be better if it was up against the wall", so that might have had something to do with it. Sorry! Anyway, there we are, then. The Stig isn't psychic. Goodbye!'

I began to suspect Hammond, perhaps peeved that I wasn't researching his equine sorcery theory, hadn't taken my questions very seriously.

My experience at Fenton Ridge, however, was proving rather more useful. With swelling confidence and a growing feel for what the car could do, I began to enjoy the experience. High speed, it seemed, was rather addictive. Could it legitimately be said that The Stig wasn't just in love with speed, he was actually *addicted* to it? I could certainly see how that would be possible, and how familiarity with speed only leads you to want more and more of it.

I can state this with some confidence since, at the end of my track session, instructor Ally McLeish took me out in a racing specification Porsche 911 with a large wing on the back and a sturdy roll cage encircling its sparse interior. It made the yellow Lotus Elise feel slow and the man in the passenger seat feel sick. Again. The forces that exerted themselves upon my head, my neck and my tortured gut were extraordinary. It was beyond mere G-force; it actually felt like violence. As we powered around the track at what felt like many hundreds of miles an hour, two things struck me. Firstly, the roll cage – I was glad to be wearing a crash helmet as my head swung wildly into the metal tubing to my left. And, secondly, what must it be like to be subjected to these forces over and over again over a period of many years? Surely that can't be good for you?

Dr Rudyard Krettle, a consultant neurosurgeon, was the man I hoped would provide the answer to that when we spoke on the telephone shortly after my experience at the Fenton Ridge track. I asked him if it was really a good idea to subject your brain to such extreme forces.

'Our brain is actually pretty well protected by protective tissue and the layer of cerebral spinal fluid that surrounds it,' Dr Krettle noted. 'It can take reasonable shocks, the kind that a human would get "in the wild" if we still lived like early man. Running, jumping, falling over, using a trampoline … if early man had a trampoline which, in all probability, he didn't. I don't know, I'm a doctor not a historian.'

Dr Krettle went on to explain that the problem for mankind is that we have invented ways of exposing ourselves to forces far greater than the brain's protection was designed to withstand:

'Obviously, early man could run about a bit but what he couldn't do was jump into a Bugatti Veyron Super Sport and drive from 0 to 62 miles per hour in 2.5 seconds. Not that I've ever heard, anyway. You might want to check that.'

However, as man has confected ever-faster speed machines, our brains and bodies have proven surprisingly able to cope with these new forces, as Dr Krettle reminded me: 'In Victorian times, it was believed that travelling at high speed would result in forces strong enough to crush you. Fortunately, that turned out to be bollocks. Which is why we now have the Aston Martin V12 Vantage. So, actually, speed isn't really a problem for us. And lateral forces are fine, up to a point. But what you're asking is, would prolonged exposure to Gs be bad for you? In principle, no. Forces are fine. It's short, sharp impacts that are bad for us. You look at the woodpecker. It's designed to be able to hammer its stupid little face into a tree over and over again because its brain is tightly packed into a thick skull with a spongy layer to protect it. We don't have that, but we are able to drive a Ferrari 599 GTO at up to 208 miles per hour. We're fine for that. The woodpecker has no call for it. Besides, how would it steer and operate the pedals? Unless we were talking about a woodpecker that was the size of a man. That I could see. I'm pretty confident the woodpecker would be able to operate the paddle shift gearbox using its wing tips and we have to assume it would have the strength in its legs necessary to depress the brake and accelerator. Plus, there's no manual clutch to worry about, so that's got to be a boon for the woodpecker. Yes, I think it would be technically feasible for a woodpecker to drive a front-engined supercar, but would it want to? We simply don't know. I would add that if you're embarking on this project and working up to the Ferrari, I'd think *very* carefully before putting such a bird into cars like Bentley Continental GTs or Jaguar XFRs with wooden interior trim. I think I can say with confidence that a woodpecker would instinctively make a complete bloody mess of the dashboard.'

Dr Krettle seemed to have become rather distracted with his deranged birds-in-cars theories and I bade him goodbye. Despite his irrelevant drivel, I was seeing things with more clarity than ever. I had learned that speed was addictive and that, in all probability, The Stig was hooked. As far as I could fathom, repeated exposure to the extremes of speed didn't automatically mean any harmful effects in the long term. I thought The Stig's character was shaped by other factors, but that his desire to drive as often and as fast as possible was simply because he was having fun.

10

STIG FOOD

I felt as if I had got a small but important insight into what it is like to be The Stig and, in particular, into the manifest joys of driving a car at a considerable speed. It then struck me that there were other known elements of The Stig's character that still needed further research and, as I mulled upon these, I remembered something that was said to me when I was researching my best-selling work, *Gordon Ramsay: A Very Wrinkled Genius* – 'A man is defined by what he eats.'

When I had visited the *Top Gear* studio a few weeks earlier, I had noticed the professionally run catering facilities, which amounted to a small, wheeled cabin hooked up to a rather shabby Mitsubishi 4x4 – essentially the kind of outfit that might be found dispensing burgers and cups of tea in a lay-by next to a busy A-road.

I observed it from afar, parked some distance away across the other side of the test track ('That's deliberate,' one researcher said to me, 'because of the smell') and when I overheard a runner asking the presenters what they would like to order for lunch, I was intrigued to know what was dispensed from this seemingly rudimentary facility.

'I'd like to eat a swan one day,' Clarkson said. 'So, yes, swan if they've got it.'

'Nothing with bits in,' Hammond requested.

James May asked for a 'steak and kidney pie if there's one going'.

I noted that, ten minutes later, the same runner walked past with a tray bearing three plates of identical grey mush. The question was, what would The Stig have for his lunch? The answer, on this occasion, was nothing. I never saw him eat, nor indeed drink, for the entire time I was on location. Yet in various *Top Gear* books, magazines and studio links it is suggested that The Stig has a hearty and curious appetite, most especially for raw meat. Was this true, and what did it say about him?

I decided to approach the studio catering van for myself, making the long walk towards the increasingly choking smell of burnt fat until I was standing in front of the van's counter being barked at by a lady identified only as 'Irene'.

'What do you want?' she shouted, idly scratching with an ungloved hand the tower of violently orange hair piled upon her head.

I explained why I was at the studio and asked if The Stig ever ate from her van?

'Stig?' she spat, possibly literally and right into one of the steaming pots in front of her. 'I ain't fed that ungrateful twat for years. Didn't like my food, see? Stuff I gave him, he just threw it in the air or smeared it along the ground or fed it to the crows, the little so-and-so. Then, this one time, I wasn't ready to serve, see? Still got the meat boiling. One minute he's standing there banging on the side of me van like an impatient little bugger, then next thing he's jumped into me jeep there and suddenly he's driven off. He's actually towing me round the bloody track at high speed in me bloody van – all me pots are going over – I was finding gristle in me hair for weeks afterwards. What a stupid sod. So I refused to feed him after that. Serves him right. Do you want something to eat or what?'

With some trepidation I accepted Irene's offer and with what little grace she could muster she handed me a plate of the same grey mush I had seen the runner taking to the presenters earlier. 'Enjoy,' she said, with what I presumed was meant to be a smile. I'm afraid to say I did not enjoy this meal, but I was rather hungry and ate as much of it as I could force down, little realising that it would come back to haunt me in a most noisy and uncomfortable way just two hours later.

The *Top Gear* caterer's refusal to serve The Stig made her barely more qualified to talk about his eating habits than she was to serve food for human consumption. I needed another lead and, happily, I found it when the *Top Gear* office put me in touch with Misha Bozeat, who was an assistant producer on the programme from 2002 until 2009 and responsible for finding things The Stig was happy to eat whilst at work. She agreed to meet me at home in Epsom.

'In the early days, we just tried to give him food from the catering truck like everyone else,' Misha recalled as we sat at the table in her brightly coloured kitchen. 'But he didn't seem to like that at all. I think the pinkish mush that was meant to be spag bol stood out as a particular low point. He took one look at it, made this sort of noise a bit like a wah-wah guitar, and the next thing you know he's thrown the plate about a hundred yards down the airfield. The caterer started to get a bit annoyed about his reaction and then one day he drove off in her 4x4 with the van still attached whilst she was cooking. I think he did about five laps before we could stop him. So that was the end of him getting food from the studio catering van.'

Misha explained that this ban forced her to start bringing foods from home in order that The Stig might eat whilst at the studio.

'I felt this duty to feed him,' she said, sweetly. 'I mean, he was technically at work like the rest of us and it seemed cruel to let him starve whilst everyone else ate. Thing is, it wasn't easy to find things he actually liked. Crisps seemed to work – he could put away tons of those, but I was a bit worried they weren't very good for him, especially since he seemed to be eating the actual bag. Cheese was another favourite. You could leave out a massive block of cheddar and 15 minutes later it'd be gone. He didn't seem too keen on vegetables, apart from cress. He loved cress. Although, again, he did seem to be eating the pot it came in as well.'

Misha remembered that she had some of her old *Top Gear* things stashed away upstairs, disappeared for a few minutes and returned with a black notebook. On the front was a large white label with 'STIG' written neatly upon it.

'I started to keep a note of the things I was giving him and which things he seemed to like,' she said, flicking slowly through the notebook's pages. 'Yes, see here, I was working through various types of fruit. Without much success, actually. Oranges, no. Bananas, no. Pears, no. Grapes, okay. And then this note here at the bottom, "Apples – very, very bad. Must NOT be allowed near apples again." Funnily enough, it was around this time we discovered the same is true of Richard Hammond.'

I was about to ask Misha to clarify what this meant when she raised an even more interesting point: 'Oh, look! This is where we discovered the raw meat thing,' she said, suddenly. 'I'd scribbled down this recipe for cottage pie here, look. To be honest, at this point I'd got quite worried about Stig not eating enough and I was determined to find a proper meal that he'd accept, so I'd started taking ingredients down to the studio and cooking things in the little kitchen at the back of the offices. Yeah, I remember this now. I'd accidentally left a bag with the raw mince and some potatoes in it on the floor of his room. When he'd safely gone out to the track I went back to get them and the raw mince had gone. I was a bit freaked out, actually. Some of the potatoes had gone too, although it turned out he'd just hidden those up his sleeves – later on he started throwing them at Patrick Stewart. It was all a bit embarrassing. We're pretty sure it's 'cos he thinks the only person who should be allowed to captain the Starship *Enterprise* is William Shatner.'

Misha told me that, despite concerns, raw meat became one of The Stig's preferred dishes and a useful tool in being able to attract him to work on time.

'I'd built up quite a list of the things he likes to eat,' she explained. 'Tinned pilchards, Lion bars, dried cat food, a small tweed hat they sold in the Marks & Spencer's menswear range around that time … all sorts of stuff, really. And, of course, the raw mince. Over the years, the production team worked all the different approved foods into a series of elaborate methods they could use to lure The Stig to the track or wherever they needed him. I can't remember a lot of them now, but there was Method 6 with the wafer-thin ham slices and a bearded man. Method 11B I remember, too – that was the one with a salad spinner full of Jaffa Cakes. And just before I left we developed Method JLS, which was a way of making The Stig go away by playing terrible, derivative boy band music at him.'

I was curious to know if this bizarre and even dangerous-sounding diet was actually healthy. The Stig certainly appeared to be in good shape, despite the random selection of things he consumed, but it led me to wonder what his preferred diet was doing to his system. Dr Philip Lyndhurst, a nutrition expert from The Royal Surrey Hospital, agreed to cast his eye over the full list of The Stig's preferred food items that Misha Bozeat had given me.

'Good Lord,' Dr Lyndhurst exclaimed, as he began reading the list when we met in a coffee shop near Guildford. 'Well, I can tell you for one thing, there are no nutrients in the actual packaging of a packet of crisps. Not that we know of, anyway. And in all my years, I've never seen "holiday brochures" referred to as a food. But it's not all bad. Blackberries are pretty nutritious.'

I had to explain that this was the popular brand of smart phone rather than the fruit. I probably shouldn't have put it on the list since, in fairness, Misha could remember only two or three occasions when The Stig had eaten such a thing. She had also noted that he had no interest in eating iPhones, Nokias or other brands of mobile.

'Hmm, well, that's very bad.' Dr Lyndhurst sighed. 'And I would imagine it would be quite easy for the little buttons to get stuck in your throat. Okay, so that's not good – I'd say "hand towels" are pretty bad; I'm also certain the human digestive system isn't really set up to deal with "Radox shower gel", if I'm honest.'

What of the raw mince? In the context of these other items, it actually started to sound quite healthy. Dr Lyndhurst cautiously agreed.

'If it's fresh and it's of decent quality then, yes, why not?' he said, matter-of-factly. 'Wouldn't eat it myself, but if you go over to France they're wolfing it down. They call it steak tartare but it's really just a load of raw mince. Actually, it's worse than that, because they put uncooked egg in it. Dirty beggers. That's how we'd come up with a bloody good dose of food poisoning in the lab, and there's Johnny Frenchman actually putting it on a menu. And I warn you now, woe betide you if you get the runs on that side of the Channel, let me tell you from bitter experience. You'll be spending the afternoon squatting over a hole in the ground while your wife is canoodling with some bloody tennis instructor. And they eat horses, the filthy swine ...'

Dr Lyndhurst ranted about the French for a further 35 minutes until I was forced to interrupt by asking if, in his experience, a human being could survive on the list of items I had presented to him, or if this diet suggested a creature that was not of our species.

'Yeah, you might be able to get by on some of this stuff,' Dr Lyndhurst said, airily. 'Wouldn't recommend it, though. I mean, it's not exactly normal. If you want my professional opinion, this Stig chap is probably a space alien or a Frenchman. Either way, not to be trusted.'

I thanked Dr Lyndhurst for his time. Later I e-mailed him some additional questions that had occurred to me but his reply was a 2,000-word rant about his estranged wife and largely useless for the purposes of this book. I accepted that I had found out enough about The Stig's diet for now and resolved to move on to investigating another of the better-known aspects of his character.

11

THE STIG AND THE SCOUTS

One of the more curious things about The Stig is his apparent fear of Scouts, as first revealed on *Top Gear* in 2008. The back-story is as follows: the Scout Association had picked The Stig to receive a special badge for 'Services to instruction' and dispatched two Scouts to present it to him on camera. What the resultant footage showed was not the expected festival of smiles and polite handshakes, but an ugly brawl in which The Stig was seen wrestling with one of the Scouts whilst another attempted to vanquish his frenzied attack by smashing him about the head and body with a plastic garden chair.

Back in the studio, James May explained that The Stig had lashed out because he was discovered to be 'terrified of Scouts' and no more was said.

Undoubtedly this left many viewers with the lingering question: why? Roy Kiddlington of *Scouts & Scouting* magazine was at the *Top Gear* studio on the day of the unfortunate incident and vividly remembers the entire scene unfolding.

'The Scouts arrived at the *Top Gear* airfield in the late morning and I remember they were all very excited to see the actual studio and to meet the presenters, who were rehearsing for the day's recording,' he recalls, when I ring him at the Specialised Interest Publishing offices. 'A producer explained to us that The Stig was out on the test track but that as soon as he was finished they would bring him to a lawn just next to the track where the presentation would take place, and they would film it for use in that week's show. No-one seemed to have any sense that this would be a problem.'

Unfortunately, it turned out to be a very large problem, as Kiddlington explains: 'The Scouts were waiting expectantly, the film crew was there ready, I had my camera poised to take some photos, and eventually a *Top Gear* researcher approached, leading The Stig towards us. As they got closer The Stig suddenly froze and seemed to cower lower to the ground, like a cornered cat. But a cat in a crash helmet. It seemed a little odd but, even so, we all got ready for the presentation to take place. As I switched on my camera I noticed that the researcher was gripping The Stig's arm and attempting to drag him closer to us. The director told the cameraman to start filming and shouted something about getting a move on, at which point the researcher pushed The Stig towards the Scouts and ... well, all hell broke loose.'

I arranged a visit to the *Top Gear* edit suite and was permitted to watch the original tape of what had happened on that fateful day. It backs up Kiddlington's report of an extraordinary and undignified spectacle. The Stig launches himself at the Scouts and knocks the oversized 'instructor' badge they were holding to the ground, before engaging in a bizarre, panicked frenzy of pushing and kicking until the Scouts are forced to retaliate. The footage transmitted on *Top Gear* shows the meat of this bizarre battle, though it cuts away as The Stig is brought to the ground, and doesn't show the aftermath in which he scrambles to his feet and runs off. Kenton Livingstone, a production assistant on the show who played the footage to me in the edit room, reports that The Stig was missing for several hours afterwards, before being found underneath the *Top Gear* production offices Porta-kabins 'like a trapped fox'.

Why, then, is The Stig so afraid of Scouts that he felt the need to lash out and then run away? Una Boon at the UK Scouting Museum had a very enlightening suggestion when I visited their recently refurbished premises: 'In recent years, Scouting has tried to move with the times by introducing new badges that reflect modern pastimes and activities. Web design, speed texting, that sort of thing,' Ms Boon explained, as we wandered amongst some of the deceptively uninteresting exhibits. 'Well, in the year 2000, the movement introduced a rather controversial "Computer gaming" badge. A lot of people said it wasn't in the spirit of Scouting and it caused a lot of fuss, but the other curious aspect was that it was designed by our then-resident artist, Will Spedding, and frankly he wasn't very good. He left soon after, went on to other things. I think he did the logo for the London Olympics. So this video games badge was meant to show a joystick and a tiny space shuttle or some such, but I think most people agreed it looked more like a thin man in a crash helmet being poked in the genitals.'

A link was forming and it grew stronger when Una recalled a tale she had been told at the time: 'One of our troop leaders – down in Guildford, I think it was – told us that some of the younger Scouts had got it into their heads that it was a badge earned for actually poking a thin man in a crash helmet in the genitals. Normally that wouldn't be such a problem, but then they were taken on a trip to a new go-kart track in the area where there was a chap in a crash helmet, and they kept trying to jab him in the ... you know, the *gentleman's region*.'

A search through the archives of local newspaper *The Guildford Bassoon* revealed no reports of a Scout-based ball-jabbing craze. However, I had already established that The Stig used to pay regular visits to the Come! Go! kart track in Guildford around this time. If he had suffered massive genital attack at the hands of a swarming mob of excitable Scouts, surely this would explain his subsequent fear of anyone in said uniform?

I called Steve Hampson, the owner of Come! Go! to ask if he recalled this extraordinary incident. 'It does ring a bell, but I was off that day. Yeah, I remember it well. It was a Saturday and I was in London to see *The Steve Wright Show Live!* at Wembley Arena. My former business partner Terry would have been running the place that day. He's dead now, of course. The wasps got him.'

Hampson could neither confirm nor deny that The Stig was there that fateful day at the kart track, but I felt certain that it must have been him who suffered such an unwarranted knacker attack.

The footage I had seen of The Stig's reaction to Scouts, some of it too needlessly stupid to be transmitted on BBC2 (though it is included in the BBC Three edit of that episode), had chilled me to the bone, yet I couldn't help but marvel that The Stig's abject fear of Scouts almost certainly stems from a poorly designed and rapidly discontinued badge.

With that mystery cleared up, I turned my attentions to another curious aspect of The Stig's character.

12

THE STIG AND STAIRS

'Some say that his heart ticks like a watch and that he's confused by stairs.'

Those words were intoned by Jeremy Clarkson as he cued up The Stig's lap in a Ferrari F430 during the eighth episode of the sixth series of *Top Gear* and, on the surface, they seem no less whimsical than any other 'Some say … ' introduction written to bring on The Stig. In the case of the allegation about his heart, this would seem to be the case. There is no evidence to suggest that The Stig's heart behaves in this way and, having been in relatively close proximity to the man himself, I could detect no horological sounds (though I later discovered that my digital tape machine had picked up a low rumble and some unusual electronic interference that sounded like a robot vomiting).

The second part of this introduction, however, seems to present something which later became an observable truth. In subsequent episodes of *Top Gear* – the race across London in series 10, episode 5 and the closing sequence of the self-made electric car item from series 14, episode 2 – The Stig is clearly seen on camera experiencing some confusion when confronted with stairs. It would be easy to dismiss this as mere television confection, something formulated by artful producers to provide a gentle in-joke for long-term *Top Gear* fans. Yet when I thought back to the day I had spent at the Dunsfold studio, something peculiar occurred to me. The fastest way from the edge of the test track into the dank production centre was up a set of rickety wooden steps and into the offices themselves. Yet when I had followed The Stig from the track to this building, he had taken the long way round, walking to the back of the Portakabins and in through another door that led to the kitchen, one accessible via a ramp and without recourse to a single stair. Could there be more to The Stig's relationship with stairs than a throwaway Clarksonian joke?

When I met with former *Top Gear* director Harry Smyte to talk about his memories of working with The Stig, I asked him about the stairs issue.

'Oh, yeah, the stairs thing. What a palaver,' he says with a laugh. Smyte is now a successful commercials director and had agreed to meet me in a pavement café near the edit suite where he works, right in the heart of London's Soho district. Smyte continues, after taking a sip of his double skinny extra shot mocha frappuccino with cheese: 'It was one of the first things they warned me about when I started on the show,' he remembers. 'If you're out on location with The Stig, which thankfully wasn't very often, keep your eye out for stairs. He will do them, but not without a bit of a fuss. I just assumed that inside the suit it was Mariah Carey.'

Smyte ignites a Camel cigarette and continues: 'So, sure enough, we're on location at Silverstone one time and we need Stig to get upstairs for some shots. I mean, he's hard enough to move around at the best of times but then this becomes a total saga. It's not so bad getting him *up* the stairs, but when we came to go *down* again he was totally useless; just stood there for ages staring at them. In the end, I said we hadn't got time for this pissing about and one of the researchers had found a catering lift nearby, so we stuck him in that to get him to the ground floor. Problem solved. But it was bloody weird, it really was.'

Smyte's recollections were echoed by those of ex-*Top Gear* researcher, Nicky Sproule, who made unsolicited reference to The Stig and stairs in an e-mail outlining some of her experiences with the tame racing driver.

'One of the strangest things about Stig was the way he couldn't use stairs,' Sproule wrote. 'Going up, he was cautious and slow (the exact opposite of Stig doing everything else!) and going down was even worse. We used to joke that he was confused by stairs, but to me it looked like he was distrustful of them or even scared of them! I'm afraid that's all I can tell you, really.'

How could a grown man, if we assume that's what The Stig is, become confused, suspicious or scared of a simple staircase? Was I missing something? Were stairs, in fact, not simple at all?

Whilst mulling on this point, I happened to attend the launch party for Professor Brian Cox's new range of petrol station sandwiches and bumped into James May, who was at the same event.

'What ho,' the presenter said cheerily, as he tucked into a sample of the 'Large Ham-dron Collider' sandwich. 'Have you managed to look into the physics of Concorde-based how's your father yet?' he asked. I muttered that I was still working on it and moved swiftly on to the question of stairs. Did they involve more complexity then I was giving them credit for?

'They're not really that complicated at all,' the presenter said confidently, wiping some mustard from around his mouth. 'Really, you have to look at stairs as a series of small platforms, each separated in the vertical plane, or on the Y axis if you would prefer, by a pre-ordained and, ideally, identical drop, thus facilitating the easy ascent and descent of a height within a given plan area that would prove prohibitively steep were it a slope.'

May continued in this vein for some time, talking almost exclusively in some form of algebra. All I could do was pretend to understand him and chew slowly on my 'The Universe Is Tuna Mayonnazing' sandwich. Eventually, after around 40 minutes (including a break for me to use the nearby lavatory), May concluded his lecture. 'In other words,' he said, 'stairs are very simple indeed.'

Why then, I asked, was The Stig so baffled by them?

'I think baffled is the wrong word,' May suggested. 'I'm almost certain that Stig is a little bit frightened of them. Perhaps he fell down stairs as a child or some other bad experience ...'

May's idle remark as he picked at a 'CERN-dried Tomato' sandwich set me thinking. Perhaps The Stig had been traumatised by stairs at some point in his life. How, though, would I ever be able to find out if this was the case? Just when I was about to abandon this whole issue, I had a stroke of luck.

I had been attempting to account for The Stig's movements in his pre-*Top Gear* days and was aware that he appeared to spend a lot of time karting, seemingly to blow off some steam. With the help of Steve Hampson at Come! Go! karting in Guildford, whose database of local kart facilities was exceeded only by his database of *Steve Wright In The Afternoon* 'factoids', I had e-mailed or telephoned every kart track I could find in the Greater Surrey area. Many had confirmed that a mysterious man in a white suit and crash helmet used to frequent their premises at various points in the 1990s, always turning up on his own and always smashing their lap records again and again. It sounded like The Stig all right, though in truth it told me little about him except that, without the benefit of a full-size test track to play on, he satiated his need for speed in other ways.

However, whilst corresponding with Sunil Mehta, the owner of Kartland in Leatherhead, one phrase in his e-mail immediately grabbed my attention: 'He was here almost every week until early 1998,' Mehta wrote. 'Then he had a little accident on the stairs and never came back.'

A little accident on the stairs? Could this be the root cause of The Stig's strange relationship with the staircase? As soon as I possibly could, I caught a train down to Leatherhead and had a taxi take me straight to Kartland, which was on a trading estate just outside the town. Sunil Mehta met me in his small office in a Portakabin next to the outdoor track.

'I remember this guy like it was yesterday,' Mehta said immediately. 'Used to show up already in the gear, right. White helmet, white suit, white racing boots, the lot. Never spoke, just wanted to get right in there, start lapping, start racing, start wiping the floor with people. Which he always did. Always. We thought it must be some famous racing driver in disguise, you know, like Nigel Mansell. But interesting. Came here all the time for something like two years, every week pretty much, so I wasn't gonna complain. A good customer is a good customer.'

So what was this accident that saw this mystery man in white cease to be one of Kartland's most regular visitors?

'In those days the track layout was different,' Mehta said, gesturing out of the window. 'The pits were in the middle and we had this metal bridge over the track so you could get to them. It had a ramp at one end and stairs at the other down into the pit area, right, and these steps used to get pretty slippy when it rained. It's like a health and safety nightmare, right, so one day I had someone come and cover them with this rubber stuff, really nice and grippy. Just after they were finished, the guy in the white suit arrives as usual, goes over the bridge, right, but then he doesn't know about the new rubber steps and he's wearing racing boots, right, which have extra-grippy soles, too. He steps down onto the first rubber step and I guess his foot just kind of grips more than he expected 'cos next thing he's, like, falling, and he falls all the way down the stairs. I was thinking, "Ah, no, this is just the sort of accident I was trying to avoid and this dude is gonna sue me now", but he just landed on his feet, you know, like a cat, and then he just walks really fast, like The Terminator or something, right across the track – all these karts that are out there dodging around him – and he just keeps walking and we never ever see him again. It was weird, man.'

Mehta showed me the old and now disused metal bridge with the stairs at one end. The rubber coating, these days slightly worn, and covered in moss, was indeed quite grippy, but what struck me most was that the steps were steep and how extraordinary it seemed that anyone could fall all the way down them and not get injured, never mind land on their feet at the bottom.

I gazed at the steps for a while until Sunil Mehta pointed out that it was raining and that he really needed to get back to work. It was hard not to be mesmerised by this faded and redundant metal structure, since it seemed almost certain to me that it was responsible for a defining moment in the life of The Stig.

Eventually, I left the karting facility and made my way back to London. It was time to turn my focus to one of the biggest facets of The Stig's television persona and one that, as I was about to discover, would go far beyond the way it was depicted on *Top Gear*.

13

STIG MUSIC

One of the best-known things about The Stig is his strange and rather random taste in music. From easy listening to national anthems, he's apparently unashamed to be seen on television enjoying them all. Apart from reggae. Various members of the *Top Gear* team insist that he 'hates' reggae.

'Some UB40 came on a radio in the production office once,' said one former producer. 'He made a weird growling noise then picked up the stereo, took it outside and threw it about 50 feet across the airfield. And if you think about it, UB40 are only *light* reggae. Mind you, they are pretty awful.'

Reggae aside, The Stig does seem to have a fascinatingly broad taste in music. His relationship with it seemed to bear further investigation so, using contacts I had built up whilst working on biographies such as *That Stings! The Rise and Fall Of The Police* and *Aretha Franklin: Going Back For Seconds At The Soul Counter*, I began to put out feelers and soon found myself on the telephone to legendary DJ Paul Gambaccini, asking him if he was aware of any influence The Stig had exerted on the music business, or vice versa.

'That's a fascinating question,' the so-called Professor of Pop said. 'Did you know that in the first six months of 1982 there were four UK number ones by artists with an S in their name, though of course during that time Bucks Fizz scored two chart toppers...'

Gambaccini continued in this vein for several hours until I could take no more and hung up.

The following week I made contact with a less insufferable music pundit called Yog Smarts. We communicated extensively over e-mail and Smarts was aware of my desire to find anything that linked The Stig to the music business, however slight or random it might be. Happily, he happens to have an extensively scanned and catalogued collection of music publications stretching back over 50 years, and he cheerfully spent some time digging through his archives looking for anything that might prove fruitful. Three weeks later, Smarts let me know that he had a few 'interesting things' for me, and we met at his elegantly scruffy West London base.

'I tell you what, man, there're Stigs all over the music business,' Smarts drawled, flopping down on a battered velvet sofa and lighting a freshly rolled cigarette. 'But I'm gonna start you off with the biggie. And, let me tell you, man, they don't get much bigger than this. John ... Paul ... George ... Ringo ...'

Smarts took a deep drag on his roll-up and then exhaled slowly for dramatic effect before sitting forward and tapping his cigarette delicately into a David Bowie ashtray on the scratched wooden coffee table between us.

'That's right,' he smiled. 'The Beatles. Let me set the scene. It's 1968. The Fab Four are the biggest band in the world, bar none. They've just been out to India, getting all mystical and

MUSIC AND AUDIO THE STIG HAS ENJOYED ON *TOP GEAR*

- Easy listening
- Country & Western
- Progressive rock
- Power ballads
- One-hit wonders
- *Daniel* by Elton John (several times)
- Bagpipes
- Vuvuzelas
- Cockney noise
- Foreign language versions of popular hits
- Learn-a-foreign-language tapes
- Self-help tapes
- Romantic fiction on audio book
- Whale song
- Morse code
- *The Archers*

OTHER MUSIC AND SOUNDS THE *TOP GEAR* TEAM CLAIM TO HAVE HEARD EMANATING FROM THE STIG'S ROOM

- Noisecore
- Grumble
- Grebo
- Milky oboe
- Wasp rock
- Twatty jazz
- Unusual tuba
- Sickening nonsense
- Alan Hansen
- Grunting

whatever. Maybe a bit, "Lucy In The Sky With Diamonds", if you know what I mean. But then they come back to London and back to work. Their last two albums were *Sgt. Pepper* and *Magical Mystery Tour,* right? No pressure or anything, but they've been on a roll and now they need to record a follow up. So they come back from India and, to be honest, they're surrounded by all these weirdos they've met on their travels. Most of 'em are idiots and liggers we've never heard of again, but there's one guy that comes up, like, five or six times in interviews and stories from that time. And here's where it gets interesting. He's this bloke who *never speaks.* And the band … let me remind you, the band that are the bloody Beatles, right? The band, they just refer to him as "Stig".'

It was an extraordinary lead. I had hoped that, at best, Smarts might find me a picture of *Top Of The Pops* from 1992 with The

Stig in the audience or some vague suggestion that he had been friends with the quiet one from Pet Shop Boys. Instead, here was a respected music writer showing me cuttings and transcripts in which arguably the greatest band of all time appeared to know someone called 'Stig'. This was exciting beyond belief and I told Smarts I had to investigate immediately. How would I do this? To my mind, there was only one way to get to the bottom of this matter: I would ring Ringo.

A few days later, I was driving a rented car through the Surrey countryside on my way to the drummer's house in Cranleigh. I had worked with Ringo many years ago on the now out-of-print autobiography *I'm A Bloody Starr, Me* and when I rang his office to ask for his help, I was delighted when the legendary drummer personally called me back the very same day to say that not only did he remember me but that, more importantly, he remembered back to the days of Beatlemania and a curious chap called Stig.

I crunched up the gravel drive of Starr's vast mansion, smack in the middle of what I had grown to call 'the rockbroker belt' – Eric Clapton had a place just near here, as I had learned when I wrote his unofficial biography *Blues Beard*. Stepping from the car, I noticed that Ringo had given his vast property a name: it was called *Dundrummin'* but he had added the word 'Not' in small letters above and to the left of the main lettering.

Starr himself answered the door. He looked tanned and relaxed, his eyes keen and sharp behind his trademark sunglasses and either side of his trademark nose. 'Come in, mate,' he said warmly, his accent a little more transatlantic than that of his surviving band mate, McCartney, and his hair a little more realistic in colour.

Ringo led me into a large, bright room containing some vast white sofas and invited me to take a seat. 'So, you're asking about a chap called "Stig" then?' he said, slowly. 'Oh, yeah, I remember him all right. Well, how couldn't I ...?'

Starr put his hands behind his head and leaned back. 'Some time in the late sixties, it must have been about 1967, Brian [Epstein, Beatles manager] got worried that we were all buying flash cars: Astons, Rollers, that sort of thing, and that one of us was bloody well going to get killed,' he began. 'I mean, I told him I only had a bloody Mini but he just said, "I don't care about you, Ringo." Anyway, he arranged for this bloke to teach us a bit about driving. Don't know where he got him from, but he was a bloody strange fella, dressed all in racing driver's overalls and a crash helmet, all white they were, and each of us had to go out and have a bloody driving lesson. He was a bloody good teacher, I remember that, even though I don't think he said more than about two words. And one of them was just a bloody grunting noise.'

Already this 'Stig' character sounded familiar. The Stig himself, I wondered, or a close relative? It was hard to know. Starr could not help me on that front, but he was able to reveal that the enforced driving lessons were not the last time the Fab Four saw 'Stig'.

'Quite a few months went by, I guess, and we were in Abbey Road recording a new LP,' the drummer recalls. 'One day this

Stig fella just turns up, still all dressed up in his crash helmet and his white suit, and he just sits down in the corner. Never said a bloody word, just sat there. George said he had "a good energy" about him so we let him stay. I can't remember why we started calling him 'Stig', we just sort of did. And he kept bloody coming back, time and time again. That's why our song "Glass Onion" was originally called, "That Bloke In The Crash Helmet Is Here Again".'

Starr admits that inter-band relations weren't good around this time and that, remarkably, it was 'Stig' who solved one of the Fab Four's bitterest disputes.

'So one day we started talking about the bloody record sleeve for the new LP,' Ringo remembers. 'Paul wanted another brightly coloured design with bloody costumes just like the last two records; John was talking about something to do with Indian mysticism and bloody symbolism. George didn't say anything. He never did. Maybe that's why he liked Stig so much. I think I might have had an idea about a squirrel in a hat. It was all a bit bloody unpleasant, everyone shouting at each other, when suddenly John yells, "No more bloody arguments! We'll let *him* design it!" and he slams a pen and paper on the table in front of Stig. So we all went away for a bit and when we came back, the piece of paper is completely blank. We all look at Stig for a minute and then John goes, "It's bloody brilliant!" and that was that. That was the cover of the next LP. No drawings, no photos, just plain white. That's why it became known as *The White Album*.'

The mysterious 'Stig' had created a seminal moment not only in the history of the Beatles but also in the history of 1960s graphic design; yet maybe he didn't realise this because, as Starr reports, he didn't stick around to soak up the praise that the bravely minimalist record sleeve garnered.

'The sleeve wasn't totally blank 'cos they made us put the band's name on the front,' Ringo pointed out. 'I don't know if that was what upset Stig, but we never bloody saw him again after that. He just disappeared. Bit bloody weird, but there you go.'

The involvement of The Stig – or at least 'a Stig' – in the illustrious history of such an enormous band was extraordinary to say the least, and when I returned to see music pundit Yog Smarts he, too, was amazed at what Ringo Starr had told me.

'That's frigging weird, man,' he drawled, carefully rolling a cigarette in his fingers. 'Since the last time I saw you I've been doing some experimenting and that, and this all makes sense now …'

Smarts put down his freshly constructed rollie and stepped over to a slew of records on the floor, from which he plucked the Beatles album *Let It Be*.

'This is the Fab Four's last studio album, although actually much of it was recorded not so long after *The White Album*,' Smarts explained, as he pulled the record from its sleeve and placed it on a record player in the corner. 'Now the last track is "Get Back", which you probably know, and as you get to the end of that track you'll hear this …'

Smarts dropped the needle onto the revolving black disc and let the last 30 seconds of music play. It was the closing moments of a familiar tune with the band seemingly improvising as the song faded out.

'Sounds all normal, right?' Smarts asked rhetorically. 'Oh, no, listen to what it sounds like if I play it the other way ...' The music expert firmly placed a finger onto the vinyl and confidently forced it to revolve in the wrong direction, causing a strange backwards sound to emerge from the speakers; at first jumbled and nonsensical until, all at once, a muffled but distinct phrase could be heard: 'Thank. You. Stig.'

'Good Lord!' I exclaimed. 'Was that what I thought it ...?'

'Oh, yeah,' said Smarts, flicking back his shaggy hair and looking rather pleased with himself. 'No-one's ever spotted that before, not that I know of. Even if they have, they probably just thought it was bollocks. But now we know different. It's the Beatles saying thank you to the bloke who came up with one of the defining moments in their career. Good, innit?' He beamed.

I agreed that it was a wonderful moment and assumed my business there was done. Smarts, however, had different ideas. It turned out he had been continuing his research, moving from the 1960s into the 1970s, and had turned up another tantalising lead.

'You know about punk, right?' Smarts said, picking up his rolled cigarette and perching on the arm of a sofa. 'Well, I've been doing some digging about the Sex Pistols, arguably THE most important band of the era, and you'll never guess what.

Yer man "Stig" crops up again. From what I could gather, he was a mate of theirs ...'

If this yielded revelations even half as interesting as those dispensed by the big-nosed tub-thumper from the Beatles it would be well worth it. I needed to speak to someone who was there at the dawn of punk and, happily, during research for my best-selling work *Kerry Katona: Pride of Warrington*, I had made contact with her fellow *I'm A Celebrity* contestant and former Sex Pistols frontman, John 'Johnny Rotten' Lydon.

After several slightly confusing phone calls and one very peculiar fax, Lydon told me he would be in the UK for a few days the following week, and agreed to meet me in a Little Chef on the A3.

'Oh, yes, I do like an Olympic Breakfast,' the former Sex Pistol drawled, looking tanned and alert when we met, though he was not long off a flight from the United States. 'But I don't like it when the toast soaks up the bean juice and tomato entrails, oh, no. You've got to move your toast. I usually ask them to put it on a separate plate. They've very obliging. Very obliging in-*deeed*.'

The restaurant was quiet and few seemed to notice the bona fide music legend sitting by the window, even though he was wearing a rather odd hat. Lydon looked at his watch. 'Is it 8 a.m.?' he asked. I told him it was actually around four in the afternoon. 'Bollocks!' he shouted. 'I'm on LA time! This is no time for brrrrrrreakfast!' Shortly afterwards he ordered a ham and cheese toastie from the 'Light Bites' menu. 'I hope it's not TOO light,' he snarled, restlessly fiddling with a packet of Sweet'N Low.

I steered the conversation immediately onto the matter of the Sex Pistols and a friend called 'Stig'. Lydon threw his head back and gave a loud snorting laugh.

'Oh, yes, Stig. Old Stiggy. Quite the character,' he cackled. 'Well, we knocked around with a right old crowd back then. It was all down to Malcolm [McLaren, the Sex Pistols' manager]. Everything was. The silly arse. There'd be all these weirdos hanging around the rehearsal room. People dressed as, I don't know, cowboys or parrots or all sorts. A bloke would walk in dressed up as a squid, you wouldn't give it a second thought. A girl would arrive with just gaffer tape over her nipples and we'd barely even notice. So when some fella comes in wearing a white racing suit with a crash helmet it wasn't unusual. You just thought, "Here's some fella in a white racing suit – well done, Malcolm, you MASSIVE KNOB."'

For those of us who might assume that at this point, surrounded by cool and unusual people, the Sex Pistols were busy perfecting the punk sound that made them so famous, Lydon has some surprising news.

'Oh, we were hard at work, but not on punk, oh, no, not punk at all,' he remembers. 'We were quite the gentle souls, quite the poets and artists. Yes, very *lilting* we were, lots of delicate ballads. We had a song called "Nice Cup Of Tea", one called "Are Your Mum & Dad Well?" There was a 13-minute killer called "Good Morning, Reverend Davidson, How Are You?" It was all very gentle indeed. Yeees.'

Lydon's toastie arrived. He peered at it for a moment and then took a bite. 'A little salty,' he sneered. 'Not good for you, the old salt. They call it WHITE POISON,' he added loudly, causing an old lady in the corner to spill her tea. 'Elton John told me that, the tubby little bugger.' Lydon chuckled, taking another vigorous bite. He then laid down the toasted sandwich and picked up his story of the Sex Pistols' change from soft balladeers to the spiky punk troubadours of legend.

'So, one day we're in the rehearsal room working on a new song – I think it was called "Auntie Daphne's Delicious Sponge Cake Recipe" – and this bloke in the white racing suit is there, sitting in the corner with his crash helmet on, as usual. We called him Stig by this point. I don't know why. He can't have come up with it himself because he never bloody spoke, the silly arse, but we called him Stig, that was the main thing. So we're working out some part of the song on guitar and old Stiggy, he's sitting there looking rather bored, as he often did. Ra-*ther* bored. Eventually, he's clearly had enough 'cos he jumps from his seat, grabs the drumsticks and starts bashing away on the kit at a ga-*zillion* miles an hour. We'd never heard anything like it. It was just so *fast*.'

According to Lydon, guitarist Steve Jones immediately attempted to play along with the breakneck rhythm but to do so he had to stick to a simple pair of chords and a rough, noisy guitar style.

'Next thing, the whole band's joining in. Right bloody noise it was, but then McLaren comes strutting in shouting "This is it!" or some such nobbery, and I suppose he was actually right for once. We'd come up with a whole new sound.'

Lydon admits he had to radically change his lyrical style and singing voice to fit in with the band's new, super-fast, super-noisy style. 'I really had to shout to make myself heard,' he recalls. 'And I had to make the words a lot less complicated. We had this song called "Out To Lunch" which was about going for a nice Sunday roast at a pub, but it was too complicated so I chopped out most of the words and eventually it became "Pretty Vacant".'

The sheer speed and fury of the music naturally led to a change in appearance, too: 'We used to wear a lot of pullovers, usually paired with a nice pair of cords,' the frontman recalls. 'But playing at high speed made you a bit hot in those clothes, so we switched to vests, paired with a nice leather jacket in case it was cold out. Once we started playing more gigs, our fans started copying that look and the next natural thing is to jam a massive safety pin through your entire head. Saw a chap do that once. Terrible mess. *Terr*-ible mess. He survived, though. Went on to become minister for education, or some bollocks. I never did see old Mister Stig again. I suppose we should thank him, really. The silly old sod basically invented punk.'

Could this be the same Stig that had created one of the Beatles' most iconic moments and, better yet, the same Stig that now appeared on *Top Gear*? It certainly sounded very much like him and, as I left Lydon in that Little Chef cheerily ordering a lemon meringue pie and bellowing, 'I hope it's not RUNNY!' at the waitress, I mused on these unexpected, fascinating yet frustratingly inconclusive tangents in The Stig's backstory.

When I returned home, I had a message from music expert Yog Smarts on my answerphone: 'I've found another Stig in music for you,' the pundit's voice drawled. 'Abba's manager, yeah? He was called Stig. I don't think he was a racing driver, though. I reckon he was just Swedish.'

I decided not to pursue it any further. The Stig's influence on music had turned out to be a fascinating avenue of research but I needed to refocus my attentions elsewhere. After all, The Stig is primarily a driver, and I wanted to know more about his relationship with professional motor racing.

14

THE FORMULA 1 CONNECTION

One of the most immediate questions about The Stig is this: if he is such a fast driver – and there's no doubt that he is – why has he never competed in the top level of motorsport, Formula 1?

To an outsider, the F1 world appears small, tight knit and based in the south of England. Because of this, any former or current employee at any team inevitably knows people at other teams and, as I began talking to Grand Prix personnel past and present, asking each of them if they had ever encountered The Stig in the F1 sphere, a constant theme began to emerge: Williams F1. The early 1980s. The Silverstone test session.

I was put in touch with Barry Stockdale, an engineer for the Williams team during the period in question. When we spoke on the phone, he confirmed that in late 1981 the team held a session at Silverstone in which a group of new drivers were given the chance to drive a Formula 1 car, meet team bosses and mingle with sponsors. He added that one of the unknown drivers was a mysterious character identified only as 'Stig'. I needed to know more and agreed to meet Stockdale in a pub near his Dorking home.

'With a name like that, I assumed he must be Scandinavian,' Stockdale recalls, carefully watching his pint of Guinness settle. 'Which is a good thing in motorsport. We have sayings about it: "If you want to finish first, first you've got to be Finnish". "If you don't want to look like a swede, get yourself a Swede". "Good in the rain, must be a Dane". You don't hear those last two so much because they're basically bollocks. But, anyway, this bloke sounded fast. And that's half the battle in F1 – it's why we spent ages trying to convince old Nigel to change his name to Thrust Manselhammer. He wasn't having any of it, of course. Anyway, this "Stig" fella rocks up, stands there not talking to anyone until it's his turn in the car. This is the old FW07, right – it's a good car if you know what you're doing, and this kid, well, he gets out there and turns in the fastest lap of the day, straight out of the box, makes the bloody thing fly. We couldn't believe it. And then he stays out there just getting faster and faster until we pull him in. Stunning.'

According to Stockdale, the team bosses were amazed and delighted with the performance of 'Stig' out on the track. On his driving alone, he seemed certain to be offered a contract, perhaps initially as a test driver, with a chance to make his Formula 1 racing debut when the time was right. But then, all too quickly, that chance started to slip away.

'We got this lad out of the car, congratulated him on his pace out there and started asking him about how the set-up felt,' Stockdale remembers. 'This is important stuff, you know; the driver's got to tell us lot with the spanners what needs tweaking so the car can go as fast as possible. So we're asking him these questions and the bloke's just standing there. He might have mumbled something, I'm not sure. Now I think back, it could just have easily been a burp.' Stockdale shakes his head and takes a sip of Guinness.

With 'Stig' apparently unwilling to provide the mechanics with technical feedback, he immediately lost some respect amongst the team. And things were about to get worse, when he was invited up to a hospitality suite to meet some key sponsors.

'This is the eighties, right? It's the start of the modern F1 era,' Stockdale explains, opening a bag of pork scratchings. 'It's about the money, it's about the sponsors, it's about the meet 'n' greet, all that stuff. As a driver, you can't just drive the car and then bugger off home. You've got to make nice with the suits, making them feel good about the millions they're spending to have their name on the side of the car.'

This, sadly, was where 'Stig' let himself down. With senior marketing people looking on, the promising driver refused to take off his crash helmet in front of the corporate guests, and then met their politely interested questions with a wall of silence.

'We sat down later on to talk through all these young lads we've seen, and the marketing bloke, he was right pissed off about this "Stig" kid,' Stockdale recollects. 'He's got some of the other people in the team raving about "Stig", waving the lap times in his face, and he's having none of it. "I can't have this driver in our team," he's shouting. "He'll offend every sponsor we've got before the end of the third race of the season!" So then we've got to pitch in from the engineers' viewpoint, and we're saying we can't have him as a tester either, 'cos we won't get any feedback. If the kid don't speak, he's no bloody use. In the end, we all agreed this "Stig" wasn't going anywhere in F1.'

Former Williams marketing manager Ken Skillett corroborates the tale told by his engineering colleague when we speak on the phone a couple of days later: 'Ah, yes, the famous silent man from the Silverstone test.' He laughs. 'I remember it well. We're all upstairs with "the suits" watching the action and giving these young drivers a sort of informal interview, just to see how they coped in the corporate side of the business. That was what it was becoming all about in F1 in those days, I'm afraid. So far we've seen a bunch of decent enough drivers, most of them polite young men who can work a room okay. But, truth is, no-one's blowing our minds as the complete package. Then word comes up that the kid ragging the car around out there is knocking big chunks off everyone else's times. The lads downstairs are definitely buzzing about this one, and that makes the sponsors excited, too. "Dear God," I'm thinking, "let this kid be a charmer. That'd make my day." I mean, he doesn't have to be a bloody stand-up comedian or anything. These sponsors, many of them have met Nigel Mansell. They can tolerate a lot. This kid just needs to be able to string a sentence together and boom!

Welcome to F1! Well, he trudges in with his crash helmet still on, which is daft for starters, and then he flat refuses to take the damn thing off. One of the big cheeses plugs on, starts asking him questions. Nothing too demanding, just "Tell us a bit about yourself" sort of things, and this lad says nothing. Jack diddly squat. The room is totally silent. I'll be honest, it was terrible. I actually remember saying, "Take your time, son," because I assumed he was nervous or something. But he wasn't nervous, he was just a bloody idiot. Here he is on the verge of the biggest leap his career will ever take and he's letting it slip through his fingers. It's embarrassing. God, it was worse than when we first had Damon Hill in and he told a 20-minute anecdote about owls.'

Skillett explains that The Stig was eventually told to leave the room and the team convened for the tense meeting Barry Stockdale outlined earlier. There was, however, one final nail in The Stig's F1 coffin, as the ex-marketing man explains: 'We've asked the drivers to stick around so that we can tell them face-to-face if we'll be taking it any further,' he says. 'Now, this is a big deal, so of course they're all sitting in another room above the pits, good as gold – these kids aren't going anywhere until they've had a yay or nay. Me and one of my colleagues go into the holding room to start calling the kids through to give 'em their fate but, guess what? That joker in the white suit, he's not bloody there. This could be the biggest day of his life and he's not even hung around to hear what we've got to say. Either he knows he's blown it and he's scarpered, or he just genuinely doesn't give a toss. You know what, I think it was that. Too cool for school, that's what he was. I've never seen anything like it before or since.'

Neither Stockdale nor Skillett could remember any subsequent encounter with 'Stig' as a jobbing driver. His pace was without equal but his reluctance to speak had killed any chance of a career in top-level motorsport. Yet it seemed curious to me that he simply showed up from nowhere and then disappeared without trace. Formula 1 is a pragmatic sport and, despite the power of money and sponsors, speed is still king. A driver of The Stig's pace would surely have found a home somewhere, even if not at Williams. Why, with his natural talents, was he not standing alongside Senna, Schumacher and Fangio, with a clutch of World Championships to his name? It didn't seem plausible that, after one test session, his chances of competing in top-level racing had been dashed. My curiosity was further aroused by the responses of those I pushed on this matter. They seemed cagey, evasive, even downright unhelpful. Finally, I got the lead I needed from a seasoned F1 reporter who asked not to be named.

'The whole Stig and F1 thing. You're right. There is a reason,' the experienced writer told me. 'But it's not a story I can tell. If it got out that it had come from me, I'd never work in F1 again.'

There must be someone who could spill the beans, I insisted.

'There is,' the journalist confirmed. 'He's a law unto himself and doesn't care who he upsets. He won't speak to F1 journalists, says we're "all Communists and homosexuals", but you might have more luck. He's getting on a bit now and they say he wants to ruffle a few feathers in the sport before he snuffs it. It's pretty well known that the one thing he hates more than socialists is the people who run F1 …'

I took down the name I was given, made a few discreet enquiries and dug out the best writing paper. Clearly, my carefully written and scrupulously polite letter did the trick because just ten days later, I found myself perched on an overstuffed armchair in the drawing room of a rambling old house in the Surrey countryside, talking to none other than motorsport legend, Sir Herbert Gussette-Claspe.

'Whisky?' barked Sir Herbert, as he fussed with the decanters on his drinks trolley.

I declined his offer, firstly because I have never been a huge fan of whisky and, secondly, because it was 10 a.m. Instead, I asked if I might be permitted something softer.

Sir Herbert harrumphed, eyed me suspiciously over his half-moon spectacles, and turned back to his drinks trolley. '*Softer?*' he muttered. 'Fine … here we are … gin.'

With the drinks sorted, the redoubtable gentleman settled in the armchair opposite, took a hearty swig of his Scotch and fixed me with a piercing stare.

'Have you heard of a *vegetarian*?' he said unexpectedly.

I confirmed that I had – they were people who didn't eat meat.

'That's what I was told as well,' he replied slowly, his red face grimacing in perplexed wonderment. 'Unbelievable. You're not from the *Daily Telegraph*, are you?' he asked in a brusque tone. I confirmed that I was not.

'Good!' he spat. 'I wrote to them recently suggesting that people who don't understand cricket should be shot. Bloody editor wouldn't print it. Nancy-boy socialist I shouldn't wonder. They're everywhere!'

Sir Herbert's moustache twitched slightly as he stared intently into space, his eyes burning with a strange and furious indignation. The silence was broken only by the faint sound of flatulence, which was emanating from the fat Labrador at Sir Herbert's feet. At least, I hoped it was coming from there. Eventually, I broke the silence by reminding Gussette-Claspppe that I was here to talk about The Stig.

'Yes! Stig!' he exploded. 'Wonderful chap. A real man of action. Known him for years. Last saw him when I had a drinks party here in the house on Boxing Day. Don't actually remember inviting him but he was here nonetheless. Turned up with an Easter egg. Not sure the silly blighter has got the hang of seasonal celebrations, frankly. Still, a thoroughly decent cove. Always found it a bally shame that he's ended up on that television show, the one with those three chaps who can't do anything properly. Watched it once. Absolute drivel. The tall one's obviously a leftie, typical BBC woofter; and the other two are clearly women.'

Sir Herbert knew The Stig from his pre-*Top Gear* days, but how?

'For heaven's sake, man, I'm getting to that. Keep your grammar-school manners to the bar room,' Gussette-Claspppe harrumphed. 'Now, you may or may not know this, but I was once the chairman of the All Britain Motor Sport Club …'

I indicated that I did know this and suggested that most people would know it since such information was readily available on Google.

'Dash it, man, I won't have that sort of talk in this drawing room!' Sir Herbert erupted. 'This isn't an army barracks! Kindly keep your urges to yourself. Now listen – as I was saying, I was the chairman of ABMSC, just as several Gussette-Clasppes were before me. You see that chap there …' He pointed to a portrait of a stern-looking man with a bulbous red nose. 'That was my father, Montgomery Gussette-Clasppe. He was the ABMSC chairman in the 1930s presiding over the golden age of motor racing. The finest motor cars, decent chaps at the wheel, plenty of pretty young fillies and absolutely no working classes, apart from the odd mechanic and a few staff to serve the drivers the pre-race cocktails. Wonderful times.'

Sir Herbert eased himself out of his armchair, prompting a flatulent noise that almost certainly didn't come from the Labrador, and stepped over to the drinks trolley.

'My father's passion, besides motor racing, was drinking,' he continued as he poured himself another stout measure of whisky. 'He was a stickler for pre-race protocol and insisted all the drivers relax by downing a sharpener or two before the flag dropped. He even came up with his own special motorsport concoction, The Gussette Fireball. Two parts gin, three parts Cognac, four parts whisky and a measure of Vermouth, all topped off with a good slosh of Champagne to give it a bit of fizz. I tell you what, three of those and you soon forgot about braking for the high banking at Brooklands. Old Bunty Gressingham-Sleeves liked them so much he once drank one *during* the race, as well. Crashed shortly afterwards. Terrible mess. Father named it the Fireball in his honour.'

Sir Herbert returned to his seat, bringing his glass and the decanter with him.

'So,' he said, eyeing my untouched gin and tonic with displeasure as he sat down. 'You may correctly gather that the two things running through the Gussette-Clasppes' blood are motorsport and alcohol. You may also note that under our careful guardianship, motor racing in this country always remained the preserve of the right sort of crowd.'

This was all very interesting, I agreed, but where did The Stig come into it?

'Dammit, man, you're not in Woolworths now,' Sir Herbert spluttered. 'Have some manners and let me get to my point. Now, where was I? Ah, yes, so my family had done a pretty sound job of keeping the riff-raff out of motorsport right up until the 1980s. Then it all went to hell in a handbasket, all thanks to *that man* ...'

Sir Herbert's eyes filled with thunder and his moustache quivered with fury.

'Bernie. Ecclestone,' he said slowly, and with obvious distaste. 'Oh, that vile man. Son of a fisherman or some such. Runs the whole dashed Formula 1 show these days, of course, the dreadful

Waterman (left) and Thaw (right) on the set of *The Sweeney* with a mysterious white-helmeted stunt driver (centre).

The Beatles in the late 1960s. Note their crash-helmeted 'friend' lurking far left

The Sex Pistols play live at the dawn of punk. Look closer and a strange, Stig-like figure is visible in the crowd.

Jackie Stewart (left) holds his famous tartan-banded helmet. Was this Scottishness inspired by the uncredited figure in white (rear, right)?

A young Ron Dennis (left) begins to see the value of efficiency and cleanliness, possibly thanks to the mystery figure visible at the top of the photo.

A young Lewis Hamilton gets an early taste of motor racing. Is that The Stig visible in the very back of the picture?

British racing legend James Hunt celebrates his victory whilst a mystery man in white (far left) looks on.

A meeting between British Leyland management and trade union officials, in 1973. Is that the mysterious 'Mr Stig', slightly obscured from view?

Designer Alec Issigonis (hand on car) celebrates the start of Mini production. Look closely to the back of the crowd – who is that man in the crash helmet?

Apple design maestro Jonathan Ive in his California office. Note the surprising quantity of

A section of the Berlin Wall falls in 1989. A strangely familiar crash helmet can be seen in the crowd.

swine. Everyone seems impressed by his billions of pounds and his business deals and so forth, but as far as the Gussette-Clasppes are concerned, he's a wretched little commoner who allowed the great unwashed into our beloved sport. I mean, have you seen Silverstone these days? All the grandstands full of hideous families wearing plimsolls and eating hot-dog sausages; all the racing cars covered in the names of ghastly telephone companies, and as for the television coverage, good heavens! The BBC have got some terrible Irishman in fancy dress doing the presentation! I tell you this – they'll have coloured drivers next.'

As Sir Herbert took another deep swig of whisky, I took the chance to distract him from his casual racism and move him back onto the subject of The Stig.

'Good Lord! You're not on a sink estate now, young man,' he fumed. 'I'm getting to that. Now, what you need to do is take yourself back to the year 1982. The oik Ecclestone had persuaded all the F1 teams to throw in their lot with him, and form a sort of trade union so that they could have more power. "I'll make you rich," he used to say to them. And the greedy buggers all fell for it. So the awful cove calls a big meeting of all the teams at the RAC Club, and as chairman of ABMSC naturally I was invited to attend. Everyone was gathered in the meeting room and in walks Ecclestone, all very tall and imposing ...'

Bernie Ecclestone? Tall? The man was barely more than five feet tall and famously so. I couldn't contain my surprise at this last claim and Sir Herbert immediately picked up on my indiscreet gasp.

'Yes, I thought that might make you splutter like a window cleaner,' Gussette-Claspe chuckled, refilling his glass. 'I know what you're thinking: Bernie Ecclestone is not a tall man. And you would be correct. But, listen here – back in those days, the squirt had confected some scheme to impress the great and the good of the motorsport world by walking around on *concealed tin legs*. He wore them under specially tailored trousers and he'd strut about the paddock as if he was really six feet tall.'

This whole claim seemed rather bizarre. Surely, I pointed out, everyone would have known about this.

'Oh, damn your eyes, man – now is not the time to speak your mind as if you're at a blasted football match,' Sir Herbert barked. 'Of course everyone knew! We were all sniggering behind his back, like you do when a chap's got a toupee or six months left to live, but the public didn't know because the television coverage at that time was pretty minimal, and Ecclestone already had all the journalists in his pocket. I mean it was absolutely forbidden to bring up the topic of his legs.'

Sir Herbert paused to refill his glass before continuing with the tale of the RAC Club meeting.

'So, we're all at this bally meeting, and that dreadful little oik says that now he's taken over the sport, we all need to think up new ways of making the racing more exciting so it can be sold on television around the world,' he remembers. 'Well, naturally I sat there in a dignified silence and refused to utter a word. The team bosses, having caught the scent of a few pounds, shillings and pence, however, were throwing suggestions in, but mostly rubbish. In fact, the only good idea came from my fellow committee member, Percy Framlingham-Soames, who was rather squiffy. He suggested a variation on a Le Mans-style start, whereby the drivers had to down a yard of ale before running to their cars. "That one's got legs, Ecclestone!" I shouted. "Tin ones!" at which point Percy fell off his chair and was evicted from the meeting. Well, the frightful oaf Ecclestone isn't happy. He calls for silence and then says something about "dragging the sport into the twentieth century". I remember him mewling on about F1 being "a show" and insisting that it needed "more theatre", and then he clanked over to an easel in the corner and whipped off the sheet covering it to reveal a drawing of the most outrageous looking Formula 1 machine. It was a brilliant white, and it had huge wings and fins projecting from the sides, like some sort of bally spaceship. It was all quite absurd. "This'll get the kids watching," I recall him saying, as he jabbed at the board and foamed with excitement like a rabid dog. Then he wobbled towards us, ranting something about how "every show needs a star". It was all quite distasteful and utterly baffling, but the silly fool wouldn't stop, oh dear me, no. "My theatre needs a star," he jabbered. "Now, which of you lot will give me a star?" and he pointed at all the team bosses in turn.'

Sir Herbert drained his glass once more and resumed his story.

'Well, all the F1 chaps were quite taken aback. The Ferrari lot said nothing, of course, but then that's just typical of Johnny Foreigner, isn't it? Perfectly capable of speaking English when the mood takes them, but when the chips are down they always pretend they can't understand a word. So, there's a moment of silence and then one of the other team bosses, I forget who, he pipes up and says he's got just the fellow. Car control like you've never seen, he claimed, and dressed all in white, just like the car in the drawing. He'll blow away the field, this chap said, and become the biggest star you've ever had. Ecclestone is clearly interested, but he says he wants his new car design to be tested in complete secrecy. "This driver," he asks, in that dreadful Cockney way of his. "Can he be trusted to keep his trap shut?" Fellow from the team is very pleased with himself. "Keep his trap shut, Bernie?" I remember him saying. "It's better than that, he can't get it open!" I forget what happened next – I might have slipped out to get another large Scottish wine – but it was agreed that this new driver would turn up at Brands Hatch to test the prototype of Ecclestone's ludicrous new design.'

Sir Herbert refilled his glass once more and politely ignored the flatulent noises that were almost certainly not coming from the Labrador, on account of the dog having waddled from the room some minutes earlier.

'Well, I wasn't going to let all this new car business happen behind my back,' Gussette-Clasppe continued. 'So, on the appointed day, I was driven down to Brands to see what was what. Well, in real life the car is even more ridiculous – it looks like a blasted cartoon from *The Eagle* comic or some such. And there, too, walking through the pits towards it, is this chap dressed in a white racing suit and helmet. I was going to have a word with him but he's plainly a man of action. Jumps straight into the car, the lower orders that are gathered around it make the engine fire, and away he goes.'

For the sake of clarity, I asked if this was The Stig.

'For the love of God, man, you're not ordering gravy in Weston-super-Mare now!' Sir Herbert exploded. 'Of course it was the bloody Stig. And I'll tell you what, he was making that car absolutely fly. All the bigwigs from all the teams are there and they were all as impressed as I was. As soon as this fellow set a new lap record, he'd go and beat it on the next lap, and so on. The stopwatch could hardly keep up. And he's doing all this even though the car clearly has dreadful handling, thanks to all those wings and fins that are stuck to the car for show. It was terribly impressive. Of course, the buffoon Ecclestone was beside himself because his grubby little plan was working, and he was no doubt imagining the white car and driver all covered in ghastly stickers advertising tripe and brown beer and what-have-you. So, as the car comes back to the garage he jumps off the pit wall and goes clanking towards it in a state of high excitement. Well, that's where it all went terribly wrong, you see ...'

Sir Herbert took a gulp of Scotch and began chuckling heartily to himself.

'Oh, it was terribly amusing,' he continued, struggling to speak through his own mirth. 'The awful man ran towards the moving car like a bally lunatic. Stig didn't have time to stop, and one of those bloody huge wings simply sliced off Ecclestone's lower legs!'

At this point, Sir Herbert could continue no more, descending into peals of laughter that eventually became a coughing fit and a stout rattle of flatulence that absolutely could not be blamed on the dog.

'Forgive me,' he said eventually, wiping tears from his bloodshot eyes. 'It really was frightfully funny. One of the tin legs ended up on the pit wall, the other clattered into one of the garages, and there's Ecclestone himself standing in the pit lane at his true height with these huge trousers trailing across the ground, totally humiliated. He was *furious*. Well, the cat was out of the bag on the false legs, and he could never go back to wearing them again. Of course, Ecclestone isn't one to forget a bad turn and he vowed that for as long as he was in charge of the sport, The Stig would never race in Formula 1 again.'

Sir Herbert paused to drain the last of the decanter's contents into his glass, dabbed at his bulbous nose with a handkerchief and sat back in his wingback.

'It was a bloody shame, if you ask me,' he mumbled. 'Instead of banning The Stig, I'd have given him a bloody peerage. Better than that lot they give gongs to these days. Have you ever watched *Question Time*? Panel's full of idiots with titles they've been given by bloody socialists in government. Mincers and lesbians, the lot of them ...'

With that, Sir Herbert Gussette-Clasppe slipped gently into a mid-morning nap. I left him snoring noisily in his armchair and returned home to consider my next line of investigation.

Out of interest, I fired an official enquiry to Formula 1 Management asking if they could confirm the story I had just been told about their founder figure.

The response from their press office was swift and to the point: 'Mr Ecclestone has no knowledge of such an incident and reminds you that he has always been of perfectly adequate height.'

I remained intrigued by The Stig's relationship with motor-sport, which was why I decided to make contact with one of racing's most enduring and respected figures.

15

THE FORMULA 1 CONNECTION PART 2

Don Wembley is a true legend within the motor-racing world, having been involved in all branches of the sport for more than 40 years. As he said himself when we first spoke on the phone, 'I've run more teams than you've had hot dinners ... assuming you've had no more than 17 hot dinners.'

Now retired, but with a keen mind and twinkling eyes behind his famous thick spectacles, Wembley invited me to his handsome home in the countryside near Esher. The venerable team manager made us each a cup of tea and, as he did, I asked if The Stig could have flourished in other branches of motorsport beyond Formula 1.

'Well, yes, he could have done,' Wembley began. 'But why would he? Thing is, maybe you don't realise how influential The Stig was in F1 itself. Just because he wasn't on the track, doesn't mean he wasn't making a difference in other ways.'

Wembley led me through to his conservatory and we sat down on a pair of cane-framed easy chairs.

'So you've heard about the famous Williams test session?' he began, idly outstretching his fingers to stroke the head of his faithful terrier, Bernie. 'Well, Formula 1 is a small world, so we all got to hear about that one pretty quickly. Everyone likes a good bit of gossip and, to be honest, a lot of the other teams found it pretty funny that the Williams lot had found this hot-shot driver but he was useless to them because he couldn't bloody talk. But I'd been in the sport a lot longer than most and everything about this fellow rang a bell. Then I heard his name and I knew I wasn't wrong. It was a guy we'd had at Tyrrell [racing team] in the sixties, I was sure of it. He was one of our van drivers, and he was called Stig.'

Wembley took a gulp of tea, giving me time to let this news sink in. 'Peculiar man, I must say. Never spoke, never came to the pub with us – you'd almost call him antisocial, but by God if you wanted a part collected from 40 miles away in double-quick time, he was the bloke you'd send. A demon behind the wheel, he was. We used to joke that he wore the crash helmet the whole time because he thought he was in the Monaco Grand Prix, even though he was actually driving a Commer van around Ockham.'

Wembley adjusted his glasses and took another sip of tea before getting to the really interesting part of the story.

'Around this time, we hired another van driver at the team, a young chap called John. Now he was another unusual gentlemen. He was what we came to know as a "rastafarian", except he was as white as you or me and he was from somewhere round here, in Surrey. He had this dreadlock hairstyle and he liked listening to this reggae music; both very unusual things at this point in the sixties. I never minded it much myself – I thought it sounded quite relaxing, but our other van man, Stig, he hated this music. Absolutely *hated* it. If they were in the goods bay and young John put on that Caribbean sound, Stig would go crazy. They really were total opposites. Stig was fast and precise and never spoke. John was slow and a bit sloppy and he just liked to sit back and smoke a rather pungent cigarette with his reggae LPs playing. Turns out, our man Stig is not so daft under the white lid. He realises he's got to work with John, so he starts ever so subtly trying to change him – by exposing him to a totally opposite influence. And what's the absolute opposite to the laid-back, sun-kissed, mellow, taking-it-easy attitude that John has somehow picked up from reggae?'

Wembley paused and stared at me through his thick spectacles for a moment. I confessed that I wasn't sure what this diametric opposite would be.

'It's obvious, isn't it?' Wembley smiled. 'Scottish.'

So it was that, according to Don Wembley, the strange Stig character began filling the Tyrrell team's goods bay with shortbread, porridge and tiny dolls wearing kilts inside little plastic tubes.

'But it went even further than that,' the F1 stalwart continued. 'John would stick his reggae on the record player and, when he wasn't looking, Stig would replace it with an LP of

Fulton Mackay reading out a bitter winter weather forecast. And the damnedest thing, it actually worked! John slowly began to lose the laid-back attitude and become upright and conscientious. His speech went from relaxed and slow to clipped and uptight. Before you knew it, the dreadlocks and the enormous tea cosy hat had gone, replaced by a tartan cap and tartan trousers. He became, to all intents and purposes, a Scotsman. And in doing so, it unlocked his inner speed. Suddenly, it was a straight fight as to who was the fastest van driver on our books, John or Stig. Except John didn't call himself John any more. He called himself Jackie. That was him from then on. Sensible, corporate, safety-conscious Jackie. Jackie Stewart. The world's most Scottish man. One day, we decided to give him a chance driving a racing car and next thing he's in the big time and a three-time F1 world champion. It's funny how few people realise he's not actually Scottish. And he never would have been if it wasn't for a van driver called Stig, who hated reggae.'

Wembley chuckled to himself at the memory, whilst I sat quite mute at the scale of this revelation. Was it *The Stig* who had effected such a radical transformation on one of the world's greatest racing drivers and a very prominent, very Scottish force in motorsport to this day? It seemed certain that it had to be.

'Oh, it sounds strange, but I think it was him, all right,' Wembley confirmed. 'Here, let me get a pen and pad,' he continued. 'If you think that's where his influence ends, I've got some people you should talk to who can tell you otherwise ...'

Wembley handed me a scrawled list and told me these were the people to speak to if I wanted to learn more about The Stig's role in top level motorsport. I thanked him for his help and headed back to London. As soon as I was back in my office, I set about tracking down the names on the piece of paper, starting with one which was accompanied by the words 'Ron' and 'man in white'. The person I needed to speak to was a retired mechanic called Peter Groat.

A few days later, I met Groat at his home in Esher. Although well into his seventies, he had a lively memory of his time working at the Brabham team in the late 1960s, and reacted immediately when I read him Don Wembley's enigmatic words.

'Oh, yes,' Groat chuckled, brushing the sleeve of his cardigan. 'He means Ron Dennis. Mr McLaren, as he is now. You may know of him. Incredibly precise about everything. Hates mess. They call him anal about detail and obsessive about cleanliness. But, let me tell you, it wasn't always like that. He joined us at Brabham in 1968 or 1969, so I guess he would have been about 20. He was quite the clown in those days. Always larking around, playing practical jokes. Great fun, of course, but not much use in the workshop. He was a nice chap, but you couldn't rely on him to do a decent bit of work or see things through; he preferred to muck about or do a slapdash job. "Shoddy Ron" we called him.'

It was surprising to learn that Dennis seemed little more than an amiable prankster with no great future ahead of him until, according to Peter Groat, he had a revelation. 'This was in about

1970 I would guess, and Ron had been made to work late at the factory because, as usual, he hadn't done something properly and we had a race coming up. The next morning, the rest of us come in and, to our surprise, not only is Ron already there, bright and early, but the whole place is spotless. This was a chap who left a trail of spilt brake fluid, screws and oily fingerprints wherever he went, and suddenly he's tidied the entire workshop. You could have eaten your dinner off the floor. Mind you, I think Ron did sometimes. Mucky bugger, he was.'

Groat reported that he and his colleagues quizzed Dennis on what might have brought about this sudden change in outlook, and were rather bemused by what they were told. 'He said it was close to midnight; he was the only one in the factory and he turned around to see this figure standing there, dressed in a white racing overall and a white crash helmet,' Groat remembered. 'Ron says this chap just stood there, a pristine white figure amongst all the muck and grime of the workshop, and it gave him a revelation: things didn't have to be dirty and oily in motorsport. Well, we all laughed at him – I suppose we thought it was another of his wind-ups, but he started to take this very seriously. You might say he even became a bit obsessed by it. Suddenly, he couldn't abide mess and dirt and he was forever cleaning up after everyone. He started to talk differently, too, always going on about "excellence" and such like. To be honest, we thought he was a bit crackers, but then he left to start his own team and, before you know it, he's running McLaren and the rest is history. I often wonder if he'd be doing that if he was still that daft, scruffy begger I knew in the old days. I saw him at the British Grand Prix a few years ago – shirt ironed, shoes as shiny as you like, and I almost went up to him and said, "Oi! I still remember when you sneezed on your own sandwich and then ate it, you mucky sod!" but I didn't. It would have been a bit rude.'

Could this strange and pristine figure in white have been The Stig? The Stig's father? An older cousin, perhaps? It was hard to know. But it was possible that The Stig had in some way changed the course of British motorsport for ever.

'The bloody silver needs cleaning again,' Groat grumbled, so I wished him well and set my sights on the next name on Don Wembley's list: Archie Beaumont.

Beaumont was sports correspondent for irreverent 1970s magazine *Bonkers!* I was able to track him down to a golf club bar near Haslemere, where he agreed to meet me for a chat. An internet search had already revealed that Beaumont was famously good friends with legendary British racing driver, James Hunt, and when we meet at the nineteenth hole on a wet Tuesday afternoon, he launches immediately into several anecdotes about the late World Champion, all of them unprintable, unintelligible or physically impossible.

I buy the veteran reporter another large gin and tonic and he settles his portly frame back in his chair as he alights on the story he thinks will interest me most.

'So, James had joined McLaren in 1976 and it had been a funny old season really,' Beaumont huffs, topping up his drink with a small bottle of Gordon's he appears to have brought from home. 'He was having a bloody good ding-dong with Lauda but then he'd been disqualified from a couple of races, Lauda had his smash in Germany [an enormous accident at the Nürburgring which almost claimed the Austrian driver's life] and what with this, that and the other, I think James was rather downcast at times.'

Beaumont notes that Lauda recovered quickly from his injuries and returned to racing, which meant that as the season reached its finale in Japan it was still a straight fight between Hunt and the Austrian for the Drivers' Championship.

'Before the last race, James went to Japan early to get in some R&R,' Beaumont explained. 'By which I mean, "rogering" and "more rogering". Problem was, he basically realised that all this Drivers' Championship stuff was quite stressful and annoying, and he would rather spend more time practising his shagging and drinking. I honestly think he'd almost given up on motorsport.'

That is until the eve of the final race when, as Beaumont tells it, Hunt had shooed a coach-load of air hostesses from his hotel suite and was slumped in a drunken stupor on a sofa.

'So, apparently, he's barely conscious when he notices this figure coming through the door and, as it comes into focus, it's a chap dressed all in a white race suit with a white crash helmet on,' the ample sports expert explains. 'Well, James is convinced it's an angel. A sort of motor-racing angel, I suppose. And he takes it as a sign that he's got to pull himself together for this last big push. When he told me this, I asked around and other people in the hotel had seen this same chap, so it wasn't his imagination and I'm pretty sure it wasn't a bloody angel, either, but we let James keep thinking that it was! That weekend, the race is just dreadful, raining so hard you can barely see – Lauda and some of the other drivers actually threw in the towel it was that bad but James, he just kept at it, brought it home in third, which was all he needed to be champ. Truth is, I don't think he'd have been so brave without that "angel" or whatever the hell it was.'

Beaumont reminds me that this was Hunt's only F1 world championship. He also reminds me that it is my round. Again.

Could the man in white in that Tokyo hotel room have been related to The Stig? Perhaps even The Stig himself? Beaumont was unsure.

'He's that chap off the television, isn't he?' he mumbles. 'Hangs around with those two idiots and that Bristolian lady? I couldn't really say. Don't really watch it myself, not since my TV got wine in it.'

I left Beaumont to finish his drink and the bottle of other drink in his coat pocket, in order to seek out the third and final name on the list Don Wembley had given me. The person I was after was called Mark McTrevish, and the note next to his name rather curiously said, 'Ham accountancy' and 'Lewis'.

McTrevish turned out to be a sports physio and I persuaded him to talk to me on the phone from his gym in Chobham.

'This is about Lewis Hamilton, isn't it?' he says, cautiously. 'Not a lot of people know this, but as a very young kid, all Lewis was interested in was maths. Maths this, maths that – if you asked him what he wanted to be when he grew up he would say, "An accountant, an actuary or something to do with book keeping." He'd probably be working on your taxes right now if it wasn't for a chance trip to a kart track.'

As McTrevish tells it, Hamilton's father had taken Lewis with him on a business trip to Surrey and was looking to amuse the maths-obsessed six year old between meetings.

'Normally, he'd just give him a pen, a double entry ledger and a solar-powered calculator and little Lewis would have been happy, but I think his dad wanted to get his nose out of those numbers and columns and *My First VAT Return* books,' McTrevish reports. 'He spotted a kart track near Esher and took him along.'

The story, since corroborated by another ex-McLaren staff member who asked not to be named, is that Lewis was initially disinterested in the karts zooming around the track. That is, until a strange figure dressed all in white caught his attention.

'This bloke is good. Like, really good. And he's out there getting faster and faster with each lap,' McTrevish explains. 'So Lewis is looking at the timing screen and he starts working out how much faster this guy is going with each lap and that's when he realises – this is maths! He loves it and that's what persuades him to have a go in the kart himself. Next thing you know, he's karting regularly and … well, you know the story from then on. But in the beginning it wasn't about the racing; it was just an excuse to do maths. And all because of that bloke in the white overalls and white helmet.'

Was it The Stig? McTrevish can't say. A request for more information from the Hamilton camp is met with the following statement: 'Lewis has always had a passion for racing. He is fully committed to the Formula 1 world championship and has little time for other activities, accountancy or otherwise.'

It seemed that avenue was closed but this was no great blow. Already I had learned enough about The Stig's staggering effect on motor racing, whenever he entered that world. I could also not forget that, at heart, this was The Stig's world and that he is, above all, a racing driver. The question was, did being a racing driver have any effect on his character? I made arrangements to find out.

16

THE RACING DRIVER'S VIEW

In the course of my research for this book (and indeed for my acclaimed Damon Hill biography, *A Whole Hill Of Skill*), I had heard others say that racing drivers are not like other people. They think differently, they move differently, they eat differently, they go to the lavatory differently (although the latter only applies if you believe a particularly ugly rumour about a well-known former driver). Could some of The Stig's character be explained by the very fact that he is a racing driver? To find out, I spoke to a real-life motorsport legend, Trenton Cleaves.

As many of you will know, Cleaves is one of the most charismatic figures in British racing. He came to fame as a Formula 1 driver in the 1970s but he has also starred in touring car racing, endurance racing and a very amusing advertisement for Willson's Motor Oils featuring a talking dog, which aired on television throughout 1983. He invited me to his delightful home near Haslemere to talk about what it's actually like to be a racing driver.

'The thing is, old chap, us drivers, we're a *breed*,' Cleaves said to me as we enjoyed a glass of wine and a warm July afternoon on the terrace overlooking his vast and rolling gardens. 'I remember once, back in the seventies, I was in bed with a girl and she said to me, "You're not like other men." "I know," I replied. "Unless other men are also shagging your sister as well!" But, actually, she had a point. Racing drivers are unique. And that's a good thing, because it gets you lots of sauce, if you know what I mean. Phwoar!'

I asked Cleaves to explain more precisely how he believed racing drivers differed from ordinary men.

'All right – say you've got a journey from A to B,' Cleaves began. 'Now a normal person would think, "I just want to get there safely and comfortably, and I might stop along the way to buy a sandwich." Whereas a racing driver sees that same journey and the only thing he thinks is, "I want to get to point B *quickly*. Because there's a girl I know who lives in B and she's a bit saucy so the quicker I get there the more time I have to get busy, as it were." Do you see what I mean?'

Cleaves's point was rather crude, but I could see what he was saying. Surely, though, a racing driver could not be defined by speed alone?

Cleaves poured himself another glass of rosé and continued: 'Of course, it's not all just about getting from one place to another as fast as possible so you can make some whale song, if you know what I mean,' he said. 'But everything in a racing driver's world basically comes back to speed. You've got to have speed in your reactions and speed in your thoughts, always taking in information, weighing up your options and reacting fast. You're in a club, for example, and there're two birds who definitely want to come back to your hotel room for a bit of wa-hey-hey, if you know what I mean. One's got a nice bum and she looks like she'd be a bit frisky, but the other one has a cracking set of Jennifers. You might have just seconds to choose and that's when the racing driver's experience and fast reactions come in. We just learn how to think and move in a split second. Of course, the real secret is, you bring both of them back to hotel. Phwoar!'

I was keen to stop Cleaves repeatedly making a faintly unsettling gesture with his arm and also to see if any of The Stig's character facets could be attributed to his being a racing driver. Would it be, for example, typical that a racing driver didn't like to speak?

'We're not always the most chatty,' Cleaves agreed. 'But it really depends. Talking to another bloke, well, that's just a waste of words, isn't it? I don't want to take a chap back to my room at the Hilton, so what's the point in speaking? A pretty filly with a smashing set on her, on the other hand… I mean, it's not a blanket rule because obviously I'm talking to you now and you're a bloke, but that's because you've paid me £250 and I'm imagining that you might have a younger sister that you could introduce me to. Do you have a younger sister?'

I told Cleaves that I didn't and moved on to another of The Stig's characteristics: his apparently low boredom threshold and his tendency to appear petulant if his interest was lost. Was this common to other drivers?

'Oh, absolutely,' Cleaves confirmed. 'I think that us drivers can get very bored, very quickly. It's all part of the speed thing, you see. We're used to things happening fast, but when they don't, we're frustrated. Any time you're just hanging around, be it in a pit garage or on the set of an advert, you're just thinking, "This is time wasted when I could be in the car ..."'

I was about to note that this rang true with my observation of The Stig at work – that all he wanted to do was drive cars around the track – but Cleaves carried on talking.

'... driving over to Cobham to see that blonde bird with the cracking assets for a bit of the old "how's your father?". Know what I mean?'

Cleaves repeatedly made a frankly obscene gesture with his hands and face until I distracted him with another question, this time about racing drivers' eating habits.

'Diet is bloody important to a driver,' Cleaves stated firmly. 'You're engaged in an activity that really hammers your body, and food is the fuel that keeps you going when you've got two or three birds on the go at once, possibly in the same room. Also, I suppose you've got the driving, which can be a bit tiring. So, yeah, you need to eat. When I was in F1 my favourite foods were melons, buns, anything that came in a nice set of jugs ...'

I let Cleaves reel off a tiresome series of euphemisms for approximately five minutes before interrupting with my next question: is music an important factor in a racing driver's life, and could it help with driving?

'It's definitely important and, yes, I think it could help,' he said, emphatically. 'Say you're in the car, you need to keep the pace up and keep you in the right frame of mind. Music can be a very powerful tool to do that. And she'll appreciate it, too. Know what I mean? Just be careful not to sit on the bloody gear-stick whilst you're busy doing the Action Jackson. Phwoar!'

Cleaves engaged in another elaborate mime which lasted fully the same amount of time it took me to go into his house and use the lavatory. I re-emerged onto the terrace and, with very little hope, pitched my final question: in behavioural terms, was The Stig a quintessential racing driver?

'The *what*?' Cleaves asked. 'Who's The Stig? I knew a bird called Tig once. Not sure what it was short for, but she was lovely bit of crumpet. Weird laugh but otherwise top drawer. Right, so The Stig? That's what you're writing about? Ohhhh, I see. Sorry, I didn't read your e-mail properly. He's the chap off that TV programme, *Top* whatsit? Yes, I have seen it once or twice, mostly in hotels when they don't have any smut channels. Which, frankly, is a disgrace. Are we done?'

Trenton Cleaves had given me a slight insight into a racing driver's mind. Unfortunately, in his case, it appeared to be the mind of an unintelligent thirteen year old. However, in between his sex-obsessed rantings, Cleaves had given me some food for thought. For The Stig, it WAS all about speed and driving. Everything else is just a waste of time. He seems at his happiest when he is in a car and able to drive that car at high velocity. After that, the rest of the world must seem rather slow and boring to him. He has to be fast. In fact, he has to be the fastest. This last point was an interesting one, and it made me wonder what happened when one of the world's other fastest racing drivers entered The Stig's world.

PEOPLE WHO HAVE BEEN SUSPECTED OF BEING THE STIG

- Damon Hill
- Michael Schumacher
- Alain Prost
- Alain Prost's brother, Dave
- Alan Hansen (before 2005)
- Sebastian Vettel
- Sebastian Coe
- Salman Rushdie
- Dame Judi Dench
- James May

PEOPLE WHO HAVE NEVER BEEN SUSPECTED OF BEING THE STIG

- Nicholas Witchell
- Nicholas Parsons
- Nicholas Soames
- Angela Lansbury
- Ant (but not Dec)
- Alan Hansen (after 2005)
- Ralf Schumacher
- Taki Inoue
- Richard Hammond
- Jeremy Clarkson

17

MICHAEL SCHUMACHER

The opening episode of the thirteenth series of *Top Gear*, first transmitted on Sunday 21 June 2009, is remembered fondly by many fans of the programme because it was on this show that The Stig was 'revealed' to be motor-racing legend and seven-time Formula 1 World Champion, Michael Schumacher.

The following week it was humorously suggested that the real Stig had subsequently been found tied to a chair, thereby quashing any suggestion that Schumacher was The Stig all along, but for me that was not the issue. Having inadvertently discovered that The Stig did not like to be impersonated, I wondered how he had reacted to this stunt. I was also curious to know how and why Schumacher himself agreed to pose as the tame racing driver.

In order to answer the latter I approached the German driver to request an interview. Sadly my request was turned down (see overleaf) but was instead able to talk to Claire Moltonoci, who was *Top Gear*'s talent producer at the time.

'We'd been hoping to get Schumacher as a guest on the show for ages,' Moltonoci recalls. 'He'd always been too busy for a trip to the UK but then, not long before we started making the next series, we heard he was going to be in the country the exact same week we would be recording our first show.'

The reason for the F1 star's trip to Britain, however, related to an entirely different TV show, as Moltonoci explains: 'Schumacher is a massive fan of *Countdown*. He can't get enough of it. He has a special satellite feed at home, just so he can watch Channel 4 at his place in Switzerland, and if he's not at home his wife is under *strict* instructions to make sure it is recorded for later. Apparently, he'd anonymously been to see the show being made several times up in Leeds but in early 2009 they moved the studio to Manchester and he was itching to watch a recording in its new home, hence the special trip to Britain. All I had to do was persuade him to stick around and come to *Top Gear*, too.'

As it turned out, Moltonoci's job was made easier by some of the guests who had been on *Top Gear* in the past.

'We heard back from Michael's people and they said he wasn't hugely familiar with our show,' she explains. 'But the good news was, he had seen it a couple of times, specifically the episodes with Carol Vorderman and the late Richard Whiteley. His assistant later told us he'd spend whole evenings combing YouTube for clips relating to all *Countdown* presenters. Apart from Jeff Stelling. He doesn't like Jeff Stelling.'

The *Countdown* connection seemed to be enough to persuade Schumacher to extend his trip to the UK and appear

MICHAEL SCHUMACHER
Weltmeister

2nd March 2012

Dear Mr du Beaumarche,

Thank you for your request to interview Michael, which has been passed to me for reply.

I am afraid Michael is extremely busy with training prior to the start of the 2012 Formula 1 season and does not have time to speak with you in the near future.

He asked me to wish you good luck with your latest work and to pass on his congratulations for your book *Carol Vorderman: Added Attraction*, which he has read and enjoyed very much.

Kind regards,

Kerstin Schmid

On behalf of Michael Schumacher

as a guest on *Top Gear*, but that alone wasn't enough for the production team. They decided they should milk Schumacher's appearance by having him dress up as The Stig and then 'reveal' his true identity on camera.

'I couldn't believe we were even going to ask this,' talent producer Moltonoci recalls. 'But I made the call to Michael's people and cautiously suggested it. They said they would ask him, but they couldn't promise anything. I was really worried he'd cancel his appearance on the show altogether. But then I had an idea. A friend of mine was a make-up artist for Granada TV where *Countdown* was filmed and, through her, I managed to get the programme's co-presenter Rachel Riley herself to ring Michael and persuade him it was a good idea. It worked a treat! Apparently he said if Rachel thought it would be fun, that was good enough for him! It was only later that his assistant told me I'd played a risky game because Michael hadn't liked Riley when she started on the show – he was very much a Vorderman fan – and it was only relatively recently that he had warmed to her as the guardian of the letters and numbers.'

With a little persuasion, Schumacher had agreed to 'be' The Stig. But was he still so keen when he arrived at the *Top Gear* studio on recording day? As I was preparing to investigate this, James May called to ask if I had received the book about Concorde he had sent to me. I confirmed that I had and then distracted him from any further idiotic theorising by asking about the day Schumacher visited Dunsfold.

'Ah, well, I'm not much of a Formula 1 fan but of course I've heard of Michael Schumacher – he was quite charming in person,'

May recalls. 'He came into the studio production office and he was full of questions. "Is that where Carol Vorderman sat?", "What was Richard Whiteley really like?", "Why haven't you had Gyles Brandreth from dictionary corner on the programme?" – that sort of thing. I remember Clarkson asked him if he was still okay to do The Stig gag and he said he'd had all the persuasion he needed. Then he added that at first he had found the idea "quite a conundrum" and he really emphasised that last word and then did a little wink and a laugh. I liked him. I suppose the main problem for us was making sure the real Stig didn't find out ...'

May's remark brought me to my biggest question about Schumacher's amusing appearance on *Top Gear*. What did The Stig make of it?

May immediately provided some insight: 'We just didn't tell him,' the presenter confessed. 'Told him to take a week off, I think. We're pretty certain he doesn't actually watch the show so everyone was sure we'd get away with it ... I'm sorry, I'm going to have to go. I was due in Warwick 20 minutes ago and I've just noticed I'm somehow driving past the sea.'

I was keen to find out if The Stig had ever discovered that he had been temporarily switched for a multiple Formula 1 champion. Former *Top Gear* producer, Sean Wellsby, ran studio operations for the thirteenth series and, when we speak on the phone, he remembers the day well.

'We'd all agreed to keep The Stig out of this one,' Wellsby recalls. 'It just seemed the safest option. It being the first show of the new series, we hadn't seen him for weeks so, on the morning of the recording, where we'd normally attempt to attract him back to the track using one of the established methods – a skip full of kittens, burning a woollen trench coat or whatever – instead, we just did nothing. And it seemed to work. There was no sign of him anywhere. Schumacher arrived, did his thing, worked like a charm. It was only when Michael was leaving that things got weird. He was taking a private jet straight back to Switzerland and, as it taxied to the end of the runway, all these crows appeared from nowhere and started swarming around. It actually looked like they were attacking it. The airfield manager went out and dispersed them with a special bird scarer thing and the plane was cleared for take off. But then, as it left the ground, a few of us saw some sort of missile come flying out of the trees on the far side of the track. It must have missed Schumacher's jet by just a few feet. God alone knows what it was or where it came from, but one of the airfield maintenance guys swears he saw a bloke in a white suit running across the fields a few minutes later.'

Happily, Michael Schumacher seems to have been unaware of the near disaster of his departure from the *Top Gear* track and went away happy with his appearance on the show.

'I think he really enjoyed himself, actually,' Wellsby says. 'The following week he sent us a thank-you card he'd had specially made. It had the *Countdown* conundrum display on the front and if you rearranged the letters it spelt "*Top Gear*". Inside he'd written something like, "I have a six-letter word this round. The word is 'THANKS!'" What a nice guy.'

Perhaps The Stig himself would struggle to agree.

18

STIG – THE MOVIE

In many ways, Michael Schumacher seemed to be the opposite of The Stig. He spoke eloquently and in many languages. The Stig didn't. He had a long and successful career in Formula 1. The Stig didn't. He had a deep interest in the television programme *Countdown*. The Stig didn't. At least, not that I knew of. One could almost say that Michael Schumacher was The Stig's nemesis.

To me, this just added another perfect element to something I had thought for a while: with his air of mystery, his silence, his ability to do things beyond the realm of most men and now the realisation that he had an arch-enemy, The Stig had a superhero-like quality to him. He could almost have come from the sharp minds and blunt felt-tips of a Japanese animation studio, though perhaps a fictional Manga version would fly (there's no evidence that The Stig himself can do such a thing, though Richard Hammond once tried to convince me that he could 'probably hover a bit').

I happened to mention my superhero thoughts to Jeremy Clarkson when we met by chance at a party to launch a new range of cakes and desserts endorsed by the ITV daytime television programme, *Loose Women.*

'I completely agree,' the presenter said with gusto, taking a bite from a Jenny Eclair. 'And so did the people who tried to make *Stig: The Movie.*'

Stig: The Movie?! I was so shocked by this revelation that I almost dropped my Sherrie Hewson Trifle.

'Has no-one told you about this?' Clarkson asked, prodding suspiciously at a slice of Cilla Black Forest Gateau. 'It was five or six years ago. Some big Hollywood producers came over and said they wanted to talk about the rights to use The Stig character. We said, there are no rights. He's an actual person. Yes, the BBC's commercial division might occasionally make a Stig-shaped contact lens solution bottle or a Stig-shaped pile cream dispenser, but he's not a fictional, trademarked creation used to sell chewing gum. If you want that, go and see Mickey Simpson or Bart Mouse.'

The Americans were, Clarkson claimed, rather confused by this Stig situation.

'I remember them blithering on, asking "He's an actual guy?" as if they thought he was just some actor in a suit. I told them, yes, he's a man. If you want to use him to make a film you'll have to ask him nicely. And good luck with that. I also tried to warn them that he was a super-army soldier but they ignored me. Idiots.'

The next day I set about tracking down the Hollywood people who had proposed to make The Stig a movie star and was soon rewarded with an e-mail reply from former *Top Gear* associate producer Ridley Smeen, who remembered the dealings with the Americans and suggested I try Bullsh Productions, based in West Hollywood. I e-mailed the addresses Smeen had given me and by that evening (my time), I was telephoning company boss, Randy Bullsh, who was having lunch (his time) in Los Angeles.

'Great to speak with you, Steven,' Bullsh gushed, only slightly incorrectly. 'You wanna talk about The Stig? Man, that was a tough project. It almost happened. So, so close. We had major studio interest, all the makings of a great script but … well, let's just say there were issues. Listen, I'm in England in a coupla weeks to play golf with some associates. Let's hook up then.'

Bullsh was good to his word and, 15 days later, I was on my way to Surrey to meet with him in person. On my way, I wondered if perhaps this very biography could form the basis for a brand-new take on *Stig: The Movie*. After all, it had worked for my earlier Christian Bale biography, *The Act of Acting*, even if the film's release was later prevented by distribution problems and an ugly legal battle over both the title and contents.

I steered my rented car up the driveway of a golf club near Chiddingfold and parked beneath a curiously amended sign that read 'NO BLACK~~S~~ *cars to be parked here.*' Inside the bar I was soon alerted to Bullsh's arrival by the loudness of both his voice and trousers. He was certainly quite a character and, after I had secured him a mineral water from the bar, he launched straight into the story behind the ill-fated Stig movie.

'Okay, so it's about 2006, I'm in England and I see this show on TV called *Top Gear*,' Bullsh explains, finally removing the needlessly floppy golfing hat that made him look like a 1920s simpleton. 'It's about these three dumb bastards arguing and catching on fire but there's also this guy called The Stig who's like a super-fast race car driver who can't talk. Straight off, this dude catches my eye and I manage to get a whole bunch of DVDs of this show before I fly back to the States. I show 'em to the guys at my company and, we all agree, this Stig character is great. He's fast, he's cool, he's mysterious. Why the hell has no-one made a movie with him? Let's us do it. It'll be a big frigging hit, I just know it.'

Bullsh and his team flew to the UK and proposed to *Top Gear* that they would like to buy the rights to The Stig character. As Jeremy had indicated to me earlier, the Americans were surprised by the response.

'So the *Top Gear* people, they're like, dude, this guy is not a character. He's an actual man!' Bullsh exclaims, wide-eyed. 'They said if you wanna put him in a movie, you gotta go ask him. So we said, cool – set up the meeting! And they got a little weird but they said they'd see what they could do. Coupla days later we're standing in the middle of a fricking disused runway with a Porsche, a plate of eggs and a poster of some old dude called Teddy Wogan. It's, like, *super* weird. Then, out of nowhere, there he is. The Stig is actually there. It was pretty cool. So I went up to him; I tried to shake his hand and he kinda knocked me to the ground. I'm thinking Jeez, this is like Russell Crowe all over again. So I get up and I start trying to talk to him about this project. Is he listening? I literally have no idea. I guess not, 'cuz after, like, 30 seconds, the guy just walks away. Just walks. Unbelievable.'

After the initial disaster of that 'meeting', Bullsh explains that he sat down again with the *Top Gear* team.

'I'm a little confused, right? I assume The Stig isn't interested but then James Clarksmond is, like, don't worry about it, he always does that, don't take it personal. So we fly back to LA and we say, screw it. Let's come up with a killer script and when we pitch that to Stig, he'll be on board with the project.'

Bullsh takes a sip of his mineral water and without warning shouts 'LARRY!' at needlessly high volume towards a man standing at the bar, before turning back to me and continuing his story.

'So we're back in Hollywood and we've got two of the best screenwriters in the business working on this script. It's gonna be the best kickass action movie you've ever seen. The Stig is like a super-hot race car driver who helps out people in need and solves crimes in his spare time and suddenly he's called on by the President of The United States to take down a rogue band of Communists who wanna destroy America. It's like *Days Of Thunder* meets *The A-Team* meets *Rocky* meets the coolest darn thing you've ever seen multiplied by 11 fricking million, right?'

A pair of middle-aged ladies at the next table pick up their drinks and move to the other side of the bar.

'But then the writers call me and they're like, "Randy, we have a major problem here ..." Oh, Jeez, I'm thinking – they missed their therapy appointment or the store sold out of those sneakers they wanted. But, no. You know what the problem is? The Stig don't talk. They got this great story, all this great action, but it ain't working a damn if the hero don't talk. I mean, this ain't frigging art house cinema, right? We need words, we need talking, we need to know this guy has a heart. So I call the guys at *Top Gear* and I say, listen, the project is going great, we're all real excited, you're going to love it but ... we need The Stig to talk. Now this is somehow amusing to them. I've got a room full of guys on a conference call in London and they're all laughing. Eventually, one of them says to me, "Randy, you don't understand. The Stig doesn't speak. You won't get him to talk, that's not what he does." So I says fine, we don't need the actual Stig for the movie. I mean, he's not an actor anyways. We'll get someone in to play him.'

Bullsh explains that the script was re-written so that The Stig could talk. He could also remove his crash helmet when required. In addition, he was now a fireman and was manfully trying to bring up his seven-year-old son on his own following the death of his wife at the hands of terrorists.

'It was a great screenplay,' Bullsh insists. 'We sent it to England and asked the guys at *Top Gear* to show it to The Stig. We heard nothing for weeks and finally I called them to ask what he thought of the script. "We're so sorry," they said. "He ate it." After that, it all just went to crap. Without permission from the guy it was based on, the studio went cold, especially since the BBC commercial people wouldn't release the rights to tie-in merchandise like Stig-shaped salt and pepper shakers and Stig tampons. So, in the end, we made a few changes to the script and sold it to another studio as *Eat, Pray, Love.*'

I thanked Randy Bullsh for his time. 'Here,' he said, pulling a sheaf of papers from his back pocket as he stood up. 'I found some pages of an old draft in my office. Enjoy!' and with that he strode noisily out of the bar to meet his friends on 'the fricking back nine'.

As I left the bar I spotted another valuable contact from my earlier research, veteran sports correspondent Archie Beaumont, asleep in a wing-backed chair near the fire. It turns out he was not asleep but in fact dead, though I only discovered this some days later, as indeed did the golf club staff.

CHAPTER EIGHTEEN

STIG - THE MOVIE

Draft 5

INT - LIVING ROOM, STIG'S HOUSE

JOHN

I came over as soon as I got your message. What's up, Stig?

STIG

John, you're my best friend so I wanted to tell you this first. I'm going back to race car driving.

JOHN

Stig, are you insane? You're going to quit your other jobs?

STIG

I have to John, it's in my blood.

JOHN

Don't do this, Stig. You're a damn good firefighter and an even better detective.

STIG

I know, I know. But this ain't just about me. It's about my son, Zak.

JOHN

Dammit, that's my point. He's seven years old, Stig. I don't want to be the one who has to tell him his daddy died in a race car accident.

STIG

I just want to give him a good life now his mommy is gone. Here, look at this…

STIG shows JOHN a flyer for a car race

JOHN

What the hell…? The Fireball Deathrace Explosotron 5000? You're not…?

STIG

John, the prize money for winning that thing is one million dollars.

JOHN

You're out of your mind. Stig, I'm begging you… holy crap, look at the TV…

JOHN points at the TV in the corner which is showing a news channel. The main image is of a super tanker at sea. The caption reads 'Evil Communist terrorists hijack super tanker'.

JOHN

My God. Those Commie bastards are going to use that super tanker to destroy America.

STIG stares with steely eyes at the TV for a moment. Slowly he looks up at a Stars and Stripes flag on the wall. He reaches for the white race car driver helmet on the counter.

STIG

Oh no they're not.

19

THE STIGGISH CAR INDUSTRY

I was beginning to build up a fascinating picture of The Stig but my work was far from done and, as I pondered which aspect of his world to research next, I continued to interview as many former and current *Top Gear* staff members as possible. During these conversations, many claimed to have caught brief glimpses of The Stig's skin, with one person claiming it 'looked extremely smooth, like pink marble'. Another said 'it seemed normal except the veins were yellow, although in fairness we were standing under a yellow studio light at the time'. There were several reports of tattoos, with one assistant producer claiming to have seen a vivid and highly detailed image on The Stig's inner wrist, which appeared to depict the newsreader, Gavin Esler.

The most interesting tattoo sighting, however, came from former *Top Gear* wardrobe assistant, Sean Belmlee – the self-styled 'man who put the Clarks in Clarkson' – who referred to something so interesting on the phone that it warranted a face-to-face meeting to get every last detail. Belmlee was working at ITV Studios on the South Bank and he agreed to meet me there.

As he continued to arrange costumes for that evening's recording of *Alistair Stewart's Real-Life Crimes On Ice*, Belmlee began to outline the incident he had alluded to on the phone; one which started with The Stig being needlessly attacked by an eagle.

'So, yes, this was about 2006, I suppose, and I don't know what on earth happened to cause it,' Belmlee recalls, flicking through a rack of glittery waistcoats. 'We were at the *Top Gear* studio getting ready for rehearsals when suddenly there was this enormous commotion outside. We all ran out and there was The Stig fighting with this enormous bird of some sort. I thought it was a pterodactyl but James May told me they don't exist any more, and that actually it was some sort of eagle. We don't know if Stig had stolen its eggs or something but this thing was furious and Stig, well, he was waving his arms around and trying to punch it. I didn't even know they had eagles in Surrey.'

During this strange, feathery fight Belmlee recalls that a gap briefly opened between The Stig's collar and his crash helmet, exposing a strange symbol apparently tattooed on the tame racing driver's neck. 'It was a sort of blue circle,' the wardrobe assistant explains, carefully setting aside a sequinned jumpsuit for that night's special guest, Kirsty Wark. 'But it had a white circle at the centre, possibly with some sort of design inside it, and then these sort of white markings that looked like they swirled around the centre.'

Belmlee drew me a rough approximation of this unusual marking. Could it provide some clue as to where The Stig came from or what he stood for, I wondered. I spent many long hours in the British Library pouring over dusty catalogues of religious symbols and poking through ancient texts looking for reference to this mysterious blue emblem. My search gave me nothing except for terrible sneezing fits.

In desperation, on the fourth day of searching, I left the library and caught the train to Oxford, having arranged to meet with David Wallingham, a professor of contextual theology at St Bernard College. Wearily prepared for this puzzle to fox even Professor Wallingham, I made my way to his lofty, book-lined office and cautiously presented him with Sean Belmlee's crudely drawn depiction; by now a little crumpled since it had been in my pocket, and also a little damp since I had been forced to blow my nose on it whilst in the library.

The professor slid his reading glasses onto his nose and peered curiously at the drawing. He made a faint 'hmm' sound, adjusted his spectacles slightly and cleared his throat. 'Ah, yes,' he said, slowly. 'I think I recognise this.'

At last! A breakthrough. I leaned forward in my armchair to await the professor's conclusion. He looked at me over his glasses and cleared his throat once more before speaking: 'Isn't it the British Leyland logo?' he said.

British Leyland? In shock at this eureka moment, I repeated the words back involuntarily in a questioning tone. 'Yes,' the professor croaked. 'I believe they were a rather large car-making concern back in the late 1960s and 1970s.' Wallingham's tone had become rather patronising but his identification was undoubtedly correct. Immediately, I made my excuses and left, pausing only to sneeze rather violently and embarrassingly into an old velvet curtain. Of course The Stig's tattoo would be car-related! Why on earth would it be religious when The Stig's only religion is cars! The question was, why of all car companies would he choose to be tattooed with this one?

When I returned to London, I e-mailed British car industry historian and archivist, Nigel Westmoor, and asked him if he could think of anything that would connect The Stig with a defunct British car giant.

A week later, Westmoor rang to say he had someone he wanted me to meet and asked if I could visit him at home in Birmingham. The very next day I was in Westmoor's chaotic living room in the Harborne area of the city, talking to an elderly and smartly dressed gentleman called Jack Adcock, one of the small team of engineers that had worked for BMC – the company that later became British Leyland – designing the original Mini.

'The management basically left [Mini designer] Alec Issigonis to get on with it: coming up with a new small car,' Adcock explained, in his thick Midlands accent. 'He assembled a small team of us and we had our own workshop at Longbridge. Most of the blokes I knew, but there was this one chap I'd never met before who sort of came and went as he pleased. We were told he was our test driver, I recall. Quite a peculiar fellow he was: didn't really speak. We actually thought he might be a bit simple but I tell you one thing, he was a heck of a good sort behind the wheel. I never knew his real name, we all just used to call him "Stig" ...'

Adcock paused to let me take in this revelation before he continued: 'Well, Mr Issigonis had been sketching away and he had this terribly clever idea that the new car would be front-wheel drive. It's normal now, of course, but it seemed very exotic at the time. Trouble was, if we did make it front-wheel drive and put the engine lengthways in the car as normal, it stuck out ahead of the front wheels and, well, it made the whole car look stupid. We were a bit flummoxed, I can tell you. Weeks we were in our little engineering cell, trying to work out what to do, and every so often Mr Issigonis would be called away to see management, always coming back in quite a fluster. The truth was, they were losing patience and if he couldn't come up with a solution, they were going to pull the plug on the whole thing, probably giving him and us lot the boot in the process.'

Although well into his eighties, Adcock's memory for this extraordinary story proved to be pin sharp. 'One night, we all left the workshop except for this Stig chap, who was beavering away in the corner. I remember wishing him a good evening; he didn't answer, of course, and I thought no more of it.' Adcock pushed his spectacles up his nose and continued. 'Next morning, we come into the workshop and we just couldn't believe it. All the drawings on our draftsman's boards had been changed and there in the middle of the room the actual bloody prototype's been changed too, so that now the engine is in *sideways*! Mr

Issigonis arrived, saw what had been done and at first he was furious, he really was, but then he studied the plans and looked at the car and then he went quiet for a bit. Well, we thought we were all for the high jump, I can tell you that. "Who has done this?" he said, and of course none of us was going to take the blame for it because it wasn't our doing so we just stood there until Mr Issigonis said, "Well, it hasn't been easy but I believe I have solved our little dilemma." And that was that. He never said another word on the matter and we just got on with finishing the car with front-wheel drive and the engine mounted crossways. It went on sale like that and the rest is history. The rest of the world copied us in due course, and Mr Issigonis always took the credit for it. The funny thing is, we never saw that Stig chap again. All very strange.'

Could this curious 'Stig' character be the actual Stig, some relative of his, or was this just a coincidental nickname? Jack Adcock could offer little explanation: 'To tell you the truth, I wouldn't recognise the bloke if he walked in now,' he wheezed. 'He always wore a crash helmet which wasn't so out of the ordinary if you remember he was a test driver, although you'd think he'd take the flaming thing off in the workshop but no, he never did. We used to joke that maybe he was The Elephant Man or summat like that. Like I said, very peculiar fellow, really. It's like what my nan used to say, "Nothing as strange as other people", eh?'

Adcock may have finished his tale about the 'Stig' on the Mini design team but, happily, Nigel Westmoor was on hand, leading us to his dining room table and a vast wad of company papers that appeared to shed more light on the fate of the mysterious 'Stig'.

'I can't tell you if this is the same chap, but there's an entry on these employment records for a Mr Stig who worked at Longbridge in the very late sixties, right around the time British Leyland was officially formed,' Westmoor said, peering through a set of rectangular reading glasses. 'As far as I can work out he was a test driver, but, apart from that, there's very little to go on, save for this card that shows he was repeatedly disciplined for driving cars at "excessive speed" and wearing them out.'

At this point, Jack Adcock started making a noise that could have been a seizure but turned out to be laughter. 'Blimey, I think I remember that chap,' he chuckled. 'Never knew his name – I was based in another part of the works by then – but we used to hear these stories of the bloke with the white crash helmet in test and development who'd take a car to the test track at MIRA or up over the Lickey Hills and come back with the tyres smoking and the brakes on fire. If you ever drove around the back of the West Works you'd see him sitting on the bench outside the design block, still in his helmet, staring at an Austin 1100 or 1800 or what-have-you, with smoke pouring off the wheels. Strange fellow he was, now I think about it.'

Westmoor considered this for a moment and offered to telephone an old friend, Harry Flax, who had worked in the Longbridge design office. A few moments later, Flax was on the line and Westmoor passed the cordless receiver to me. 'Gosh, yes, I remember that chap,' the retired designer guffawed. 'You'd hear a screech outside and some poor test car would pull up, smoking and stinking up the place, and this extraordinary figure in a white crash helmet would jump out and just sit there outside our office waiting for it to cool down. Happened all the time when we were working on ADO67, the project that became the Allegro. Poor old Harris Mann, who styled that thing – every time he looked out of his window he'd be staring at the back of this lunatic's crash helmet. We used to joke that it became his main inspiration. And, well, actually, if you look at the back of an Allegro in white ... Never sold too well, that car. Maybe it looked too much like a crash helmet, eh?'

It seemed extraordinary to think that 'Mr Stig', whoever he was, might have saved the company with his ingenious Mini design and then helped to destroy it by inadvertently inspiring the appearance of one of its most infamously bulbous cars.

Nigel Westmoor had more to come, presenting me with a sheaf of transcripts dating from the early 1970s. They detailed meetings between British Leyland management and the trade unions that represented the company's workforce. It was a time of great industrial unrest and the unions wielded such power that they could easily have brought the company to its knees.

Reading through the transcripts, it was clear that negotiations over pay and conditions were delicate and detailed, but that real progress was being made to find a happy compromise that would enable the vast Leyland empire to survive those difficult times.

Westmoor steered me towards the vital turning point in what was, thus far, a largely successful process.

In what would appear to be an attempt to sway proceedings in their favour, BL management had brought in a new negotiator of the 'strong, silent type'. The meeting transcript, dated 15 February 1973, records his name only as 'Mr Stig'. At the start of a tense discussion, a senior union official asked that Mr Stig 'respectfully removes his crash helmet'. This request was apparently ignored. The union officials pushed on with their latest demands but, crucially, also gave a suggestion that they were willing to compromise on what appeared to be a vital agreement on working hours. Representing British Leyland, Mr Stig said nothing. The transcript did not record tone or volume of speech but it was clear that the union officials were agitated by this silence. One asked for at least some acknowledgement that his comrades were ready to compromise for the greater good. No acknowledgement was forthcoming. Finally, a union leader identified only as 'Mr Mosswell' appeared to lose patience: 'This is just the sort of arrogance we've come to expect from management,' he was recorded as saying. 'We came here to find resolution and all this joker wants is another fight. Well, if it's a fight he wants, it's a fight he's going to bloody get.' With that, the entire trade union contingent was recorded as leaving the meeting room. Westmoor showed me a newspaper cutting which revealed that a mass walkout happened across all BL plants later that day. It was the start of a series of industrial actions that would eventually bring British Leyland to its knees and set the charges for the eventual collapse of the entire UK car industry.

At this point Westmoor's paper trail went cold. He could find no more reference to 'Mr Stig' nor any conclusive proof that this was the same man who had worked on the original Mini or became Longbridge's infamous white-helmeted test driver. Could it have been The Stig himself? Was it possible that he had the British Leyland logo tattooed on his neck as a tribute to the company he had inadvertently destroyed? I left Nigel Westmoor's house none the wiser. I was still rather confused as to why The Stig was being attacked by an eagle in the first place. Perhaps it was time to park these queries and pursue other avenues.

20

iSTIG

Whilst I was looking for another angle to explore in my quest to get to the heart of The Stig, I attended a party to celebrate the launch of Matthew Pinsent's new range of marinades and cook-in sauces, coincidentally bumping into Richard Hammond, who was at the same event.

'Have you found out any more about wizards and horses and stuff?' the presenter asked keenly. I said I had been busy on other matters and hurriedly crammed a sample of Coxless Chicken into my mouth.

'Shame,' Hammond replied, grabbing a sample of Oar-some Pork from a passing server. 'So what *have* you found out?'

I told him at length about a few of my recent discoveries, including the anecdote about the influence on the design of the Austin Allegro. Hammond laughed so hard he almost choked on his Sir Seasoned Redgrave Salmon.

'Well, you're allowed one cock up.' He smiled. 'I suppose as long as you ignore that disaster, you'd have to say Stig is basically a design icon. And I went to art college, so I can say stuff like that and only sound like a *bit* of a twat ...'

Hammond may have had a point. Can The Stig truly be considered a design icon? Can he even be called 'designed'? That in itself raised an interesting issue and I resolved to investigate further. On the surface this might not seem relevant to the issue of finding out more about the man behind the visor but, as I learned when researching my best-selling work *M Is For Versatile: The Meryl Streep Story*, sometimes the most abstract tangents can lead to the most explosive revelations (and, in that case, the acquisition of a criminal record in Luxembourg).

I had contacts in the design world from my 1995 work, *Sir Terence Conran: From Chairs To Where?* and after dispatching several e-mails, I found myself talking to renowned design commentator, Stephen Bayley.

My first question to Bayley was blunt and to the point: where is your lavatory? It had been a long taxi ride during which my driver had got lost, angry, lost, sorrowful, very angry and then arrested.

My second question was simple: could The Stig be considered a design icon?

Bayley sat back in his Eames chair, pressed his hands together and closed his eyes. 'An excellent question,' he said, slowly. 'The first thing that strikes one about The Stig is the whiteness of his suit – the purity of that as a colour scheme or, as one might argue, the *lack* of colour scheme and how much a pure tone clears the mind of the torpor of solipsism that can infest some of the weaker manifestos of design. Minimalism can be in and of itself when applied with intelligence and I think here, with The Stig, we see a very knowing application of the less-is-more-is-less phenomenology ...'

Bayley continued in this vein for some time, during which I was able, quite unnoticed, to slip away to the kitchen and make three separate mobile phone calls. When I returned he was concluding with something about 'an unbearable ennui of line' before, quite unexpectedly, he said something very interesting.

'So, yes, perhaps The Stig is an icon,' Bayley purred. 'After all, look at his influence on [Apple computers designer] Jonathan Ive.'

I asked Bayley to elaborate. After going off on a tangent about 'inept synaesthesia' for 15 minutes, he agreed.

'It's not very well known that Jony Ive and Steve Jobs reached a furious impasse over the design of the Apple iPod,' Bayley explained. 'The whole project was almost stillborn until Ive had a moment of glorious inspiration. I'm sure others can tell you more, but put it this way – why do you think the original iPod was white?'

Bayley was making an extraordinary claim and one that I sought immediately to verify with Apple themselves. The company replied quickly, denying my request to speak to Jonathan Ive or engage in any discussion about The Stig.

Fortunately, I was able to make contact with unofficial Apple historian Randy Frendless. Speaking on the phone from his parents' house in Northern California, Frendless is almost breathless with excitement to share this little-known tale. It was only later I discovered he was also having an asthma attack.

'So, it's 2000, maybe 2001, and Steve Jobs has committed Apple to making a revolutionary MP3 player,' Frendless gasps. 'Jony Ive is one of the design engineers and it's his job to work out what this thing is gonna look like. Problem is, Jony is British, right? So his inspiration is kinda different to the other guys at Apple. It's all about drizzle, overcooked meat, some place called Meelton Key-nez. The guy comes from the land of grey, right? So, he's coming up with these MP3 player designs that are, like, dull grey boxes. Well, Steve Jobs sees this, he goes nuts – he wants it to be cool, and grey ain't cool.'

Frendless goes on to explain that Jobs himself had some very definite ideas about how the new device should look.

'I know one of the guys who worked on the project,' he reveals. 'He said Steve wanted the player to be black, like his clothes. Every day he'd be following Jony Ive down the corridors shouting, "Look at my sweater, bitch!" but Jony wasn't convinced.'

As Frendless tells the story, Ive became so harassed by a sweater-obsessed Jobs that he eventually escaped the Apple campus for a few days and drove around Northern California looking for new inspiration. Finally, by chance, he ended up at the Laguna Seca racing circuit.

'Jony's looking everywhere for inspiration and he finds himself at this race track,' Frendless wheezes. 'Well, the place is closed but he can hear the sound of an engine in the distance so he finds a hole in the fence somehow, walks towards the track and there's this dude wrestling a muscle car around, doing totally cool things, like totally on fire out there. So Jony sits down, he starts sketching – you know, suddenly he's feeling something, like he might have an idea – he's, like, totally mesmerised by what he's seeing. But it's not the car or the race track that's got him, it's the guy behind the wheel. So he walks towards the pits to get a closer look and when this guy comes in, he steps from the car and he's dressed totally in white, like white suit, white shoes, white helmet, and he's, like, totally backlit by the sun going down and Jony is mesmerised. This dude is, like, super-cool. Jony drives straight back to Cupertino and comes up with a brand new MP3 player design, all in white. Steve loves it, everyone loves it, and the rest is history ...'

Could that inspiring driver in the white suit have been The Stig? I rang the Laguna Seca track in California and spoke to their archivist, Chuck Steele.

'I'm sorry, son, we don' have archives for drivers using the track at that time no more,' he said. 'Darn raccoons got to 'em.'

Unbowed, I called on contacts at several airlines and the Home Office. Could they find any record of a 'Mr Stig' flying to the US around that time? The search yielded nothing. On reflection, it was a long shot. I remember something Jeremy had said to me about The Stig's preferred methods of long-distance travel: 'As freight, by airship or in a very silly hovercraft.'

The white suit and the sensational driving strongly suggested it was The Stig himself at Laguna Seca that day and that, as a result, Jonathan Ive was inspired to make the iPod white, but it seems almost impossible to prove for certain.

Oddly enough, however, it seems Ive himself is in no doubt that he owes The Stig a huge debt of gratitude for his greatest design decision.

'Jony Ive loves The Stig,' confirms unofficial Apple historian Randy Frendless. 'They say the first time he first saw an episode of *Top Gear* was around 2005 when he was visiting the UK and suddenly he realised, that's him! That's the guy he saw at the race track. Ever since then he's been obsessed. Sure, they play it down but ask anyone who's ever worked at Apple and seen inside Jony's office. It's wall-to-wall with Stig merchandise: posters, mugs, mouse mats, shower gel, cakes, duvet covers, pregnancy testing kits. Anything with The Stig on it, he'll buy it. Not just for The Stig himself, but for the quality of the products and care with which the BBC allows his likeness to be used.'

If it really was The Stig at Laguna Seca that day, one can only begin to imagine how different the electronics industry would be today if he had been red or green or zebra striped. It's perhaps fortunate, then, that he wasn't.

From: Apple comms

To: Simon du Beaumarche

Subject: Re. iPod design inspiration

Mr du Beaumarche,

Thank you for your recent request. We cannot arrange an interview with Sir Jonathan Ive at this time. He is busy.

Furthermore, we cannot engage in any discussion regarding 'The Stig'.

Why not visit the App Store® to download the awesome new Mind Your Own Business™ app?

Best,

Taylor Otterburger
Senior Vice Junior President of Communications

21

ART AND ARCHSTIGTECTURE

I had already established the influence of The Stig in product design and, indeed, in car design, but I was keen to discover if he had inspired designers in other spheres. Apart from anything else, Stephen Bayley was leaving increasingly lengthy verbal essays on my answering machine covering topics such as 'the agony of purity', and I was hoping that if he heard I was still working on the design angle he would leave me alone.

I began to look at the world of architecture, searching for some suggestion that The Stig had been a factor in the appearance of any building or buildings either in the UK or overseas. My early investigations proved fruitless but then, in an architecture and design magazine, *[[etude elegance]]*, I stumbled upon a curious reference to a 'mysterious figure in a crash helmet'. It was in an article about the British sculptor, Antony Gormley.

My attempt to contact Gormley himself was met with a short message that told me he was 'too busy', but I had more success with the arts journalist, Jocasta Meede, who agreed to meet me at a coffee shop in Epsom.

'I think I know what this is about,' Meede said to me as we sat down to talk. 'Throughout the eighties, Gormley was struggling along with these sculptures of people. They were pretty good in themselves, except for the heads. He insisted on giving them a range of outlandish hairstyles – afros, Mohicans, that sort of silly central parting style that the chap from the Happy Mondays used to have – and I think most people felt that rather detracted from their purity. It made them look stupid, really.'

Gormley's style was about to change, however, and it came about after a chance encounter whilst walking in the south east of England.

'The story is that Gormley was out walking on the South Downs, not far from here, actually,' Meede explained. 'He sees this chap walking along one of the tops and, ridiculous though this sounds, he's wearing a crash helmet. Well, they say that was all the inspiration Gormley needed. No more outlandish hairstyles on his sculptures – he'll make their heads smooth. Better than that, the sight of this man in a racing driver outfit or what-have-you, just standing in open countryside, really inspires him to place some of his new sculptures in similar situations. The newfound purity and simplicity of the figures, the vastness of the landscape; they say it all came from that one encounter on the Downs.'

Could this have been The Stig that Antony Gormley encountered in the countryside that day? It was hard to say. Meede believed this event took place in the very late 1980s or early

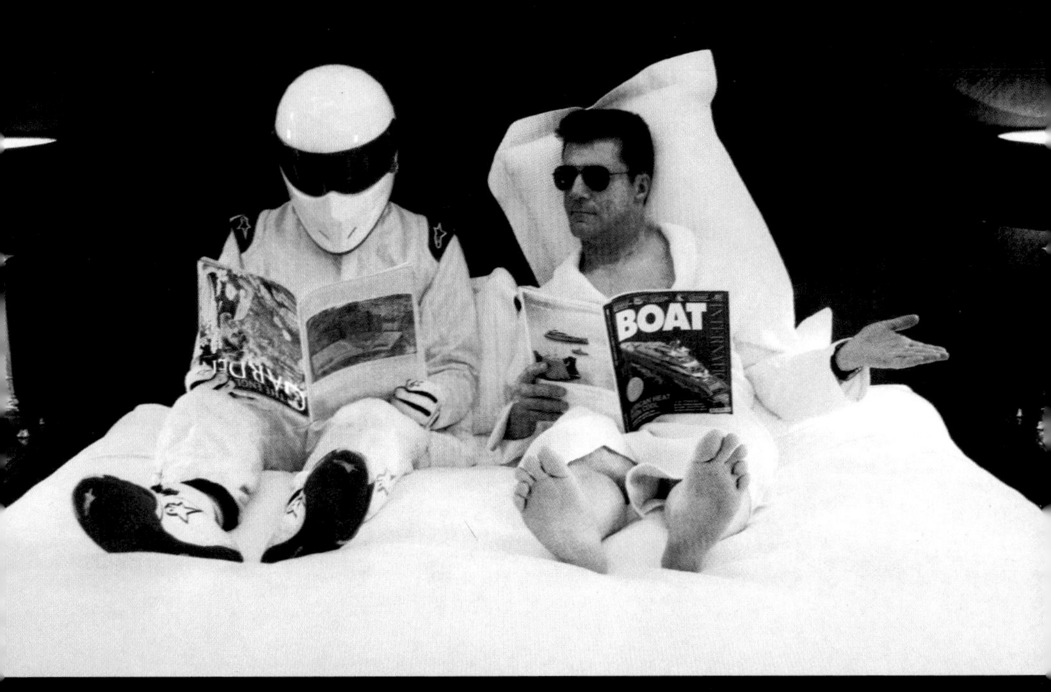

Best of friends? Simon Cowell and The Stig are rumoured to be close.

Lost in showbiz? A snatched mobile-phone photo appears to show a figure in white relaxing with David Beckham.

Party animal? A sneak photo seems to show Russell Brand back to his old ways whilst a Stig-like party-goer is distracted by other matters.

Still lost in showbiz? A paparazzi picture captures a mystery man holding the baby on a shopping trip with Elton John.

Later that day, Elton is snapped enjoying a quiet coffee with his mysterious friend.

What friends are for? This rare paparazzi shot appears to show that a white-suited figure is responsible for Simon Cowell's recent appearance.

Ouch! Over-the-fence pictures show a friendly kick-about with an unknown man in white gone badly wrong for Beckham.

'This is my chaperone.' Prince Harry appears to try his luck with Pippa Middleton, who only has eyes

Brazilian racer Rubens Barrichello poses for the cameras, but who is that driving the steam roller behind him?

The key to the puzzle? Moustachioed motorsport legend Gordon Murray.

The centre of it all? 29 Magnolia Avenue, Guildford.

1990s, an era when I had yet to account for The Stig's movements. It was not outside the bounds of possibility that he was spending his time walking in the splendour of the South Downs. However, Jocasta Meede had another revelation in store.

'It actually gets better. Wait until you hear this,' she whispered. 'The story is that after that first moment of inspiration, Gormley became very fond of the Downs and used to go there more regularly. So he's up there one day and he sees the same figure in a crash helmet, except this time this strange chap has got a great big wing strapped to his back and he's just standing on the tops, staring down at the countryside. They say that Gormley was totally bewitched by this and he went straight back to his studio to begin sketching what would become his most dramatic – some would say his greatest – work to date: the Angel Of The North.'

Meede's story sounded plausible and yet all at once ridiculous. The Stig walking in the countryside was one thing. But The Stig with a huge wing on his back? That was extremely intriguing and warranted further investigation. To find out more, I travelled to the South Downs and combed the local area looking for someone who might also have seen this curious sight. Eventually, I struck gold. Nigel Williams has owned and run a farm at the very base of the Downs for the past 27 years. He remembers the 'loony in the crash helmet' all too well.

'This would have been the late eighties,' he recalls, as we walk through the yard at his ramshackle farm. 'It all started in late summer, I 'spose. There's a commotion in one of the fields one evening, I go up there and there's some weirdo in a white racing suit and a crash helmet running about after my cows. I shouted at him and he legged it off into the woods. Didn't really think about it much after that. I mean, you get all sorts, don't you? But then a few days later he's at it again. And this keeps happening. Every few days I catch him legging it around the field after the bloody cows. God knows what he was trying to do with them. Milk 'em? Eat 'em? I don't even want to think about it.'

Williams explains that this became such a problem he and his farmhands started keeping guard around the fields where his cattle grazed, in an attempt to deter this strange intruder.

'Well, it seemed to work at first,' he says. 'But then one day I'm keeping watch and suddenly from nowhere this bloody idiot comes in from above. He's only gone and got a pair of wings on his back and he's flown into the field! He's there, swooping over the cows, giving them a right fright, and then he lands, unclips the wings and runs off again! I didn't know what to think. At that point I told the police and I moved the cows to another field under some power lines. "That'll show the flying bastard," I thought. The problem just sort of went away. Bloody students, I shouldn't wonder.'

I had heard many unusual stories that almost certainly involved The Stig but this was one of the strangest. Yet it seemed heartening to know that, whilst his desire to attack cattle was troubling, he had at the same time inadvertently inspired some of the greatest sculptural works of the late twentieth century.

And, as I was about to find out, he may also have influenced an iconic building at the very cusp of the transition between the centuries, too.

In my attempt to find a link between The Stig and other pieces of design, I contacted Sir Benjinald Rutt, one of Britain's most famous architects and architectural commentators. With prior arrangement, I drove straight from Nigel Williams's farm to Rutt's home in Walton-on-Thames.

'Jesus Christ, have you got faeces on your shoes?' he boomed, when I arrived at his avant-garde 1960s property on the banks of the river. I realised that I had. Nonetheless, Sir Benjinald agreed that if I removed my shoes he would let me follow him to the back of the fascinating property and join him in his immaculately furnished office overlooking the water.

'The Stig?' he spluttered, as we settled on two extremely interesting and also extremely uncomfortable chairs. 'Yes, I know of The Stig. He's from that programme with those three other idiots who are always setting their trousers on fire. Quite the joke in architecture circles, that is. Not the trousers on fire – that's no laughing matter; it's happened to me, and it bloody hurts. I'm talking about the chap in the crash helmet. You don't know the story about Richard Rogers then, do you?'

I had heard of Richard Rogers, of course. He is another of Britain's most respected architects, responsible for buildings such the Lloyds Building in London and the Pompidou Centre in Paris. I was not sure, however, that I knew 'the story' about him. I indicated as much and Sir Benjinald leaned back in his minimalist office chair, took a sip from the whisky he had poured for himself without offering any to me, and began to explain.

'So, it's the middle nineties, he's been asked to come up with a design for this new building that's going to mark the change of century and, the story is, he's stumped. It's really frustrating him, so to cheer himself up he decides to take a drive out to a Harvester to get some lunch. What a lot of people don't realise about Richard is that he loves a Harvester. Loves it. You show him a pub with that green sign on the front and he's in there, diving into the all-you-can-eat salad bar with a big smile on his face. Anyway, he heads down to some place near Byfleet, gets his table, makes a sortie to the salad bar as usual, but when he comes back there's some lunatic sitting with his back to him at the next table, wearing a white crash helmet. So all through lunch he's staring at the top of the crash helmet poking over the divider between the two booths and suddenly it gives him an idea. A dome! That's what he'll do for the millennium thing by the river in Greenwich. A white, crash helmet-y, millennium dome. And the rest, I suppose, is history. Except for rivers. They're geography.'

Could it have been The Stig that inspired Richard Rogers on one of his regular trips to a Harvester? Logically, anyone could have been wearing a white crash helmet in that family-friendly pub-cum-restaurant on that particular day, yet you would have to say that most motorcyclists remove their protective headwear once they have dismounted from their machine. We will almost certainly never know for sure if The Stig was the inspiration for the Millennium Dome, though of course it would be delightful to consider this the case, especially now that the building has become useful.

Since we were on the subject, I wondered if Sir Benjinald had any other stories that might link The Stig to great architectural endeavours.

'Oh, I don't know,' he slurred. 'What do you fancy? The Gherkin. That looks a bit like a crash helmet. St Pancras station? That's what The Stig looks like if you cut him open – oh, yes, he's full of Victorian splendour. What about The Shard? That's not what I call it. I call it The Stig's Todger. Yeeeees! Ha ha ha haaaa.'

It was only the middle of the afternoon but I began to suspect that Sir Benjinald was really very drunk. Still, what he had told me was fascinating. The Stig may well have had a real influence on architecture, as well as commercial design and the arts. If only he had inspired the invention of something to get cow dung off a pair of brogues.

22

THE FALL OF THE BER-STIG WALL

In the process of putting together a biography, one always sends out as many feelers as possible. When I was working on my best-selling work, *Vinnie Jones: Hardman to Bardman*, for example, I must have written over 500 letters, interviewed over 150 people and been bundled into the back of over seven vans. Sometimes, however, you do not have to seek out the information: the information comes to you. So it was that I received a mysterious communication via former SAS hero Dave McLeish, whom I had worked with on the book *Death Starts With An R*. The message was from a man calling himself only 'Captain B' and it said simply that he had heard I was writing a book about The Stig and intimated that he might have information for me. With McLeish acting as go-between, I agreed to meet the mystery contact in a room at a Premier Inn in Bagshot.

CHAPTER TWENTY-TWO

I arrived at the designated hotel and was told by the receptionist that my 'colleague' was already in room 117. With slight trepidation, I walked down the ground floor corridor and knocked gently on the door. Almost immediately, it swung open slightly and, without thinking, I walked forwards into the room – only to feel a large hand clamp around my face. Unable to see my assailant, I felt them pull me closer to them with the arm still grasping my head, whilst another hand began aggressively patting down my arms, legs and torso before I was released with a push that sent me stumbling towards the queen-sized double bed in the middle of the room.

'Sorry about that,' a Scots voice said. 'You never know who's carrying a weapon these days.' It was 'Captain B'. He was a large Scottish man in his late forties, a little paunchy perhaps, but still an intimidating physical presence and obviously very strong.

However, once his initial and rather unconventional welcome was dispensed with, Captain B turned out to be quite friendly, very helpful and worth the £86 it had cost me for this slightly unusual meeting place.

Captain B told me that his real name was Bob and that he was a former member of the Special Forces who had served in Germany during the 1980s, working with a unique unit called the British Commander-in-Chief's Mission to the Soviet Forces in Germany, or BRIXMIS for short. The unit's purpose was ostensibly to maintain a mutually agreed military–diplomatic presence in Soviet-occupied East Germany during the tense times of the Cold War. The reality was rather different. As Bob explained whilst I made us both a drink from the complimentary tea and coffee making facilities, BRIXMIS was also there to spy.

'The Soviets had bases all over East Germany,' Bob explained, as he opened a pack of complimentary shortbread. 'We were allowed to move around with relative freedom, and that meant we could travel all over the place observing and photographing all the Soviet military hardware we could lay eyes on and then feeding it back to the West. The Ruskies knew what we were up to and they let us get away with a certain amount. The trick was to avoid getting caught doing anything too naughty.'

So far, I was still searching for two things. Firstly, a sachet of coffee that wasn't decaffeinated. And, secondly, anything that might link this interesting tale to The Stig. Happily, Bob was about to provide that link.

'To get around, we were provided with specially modified cars. By the time I was out there in 1988, these were mostly Mercedes G-Wagen 4x4s, sprayed matt green with blacked-out windows and with a few trick bits. Great for covering tricky off-road terrain but not so clever on the road when you're trying to get away from a bloody member of the Stasi [East German secret police] who's spotted you somewhere you shouldn't be. Yeah, to get the best out of those old Mercs on the road, you really needed to know what you were doing. And that's where yer man Stig came in ...'

I stopped in my attempts to open a window and gave Bob my full attention.

'He turned up one day – must have been summer 1988. They said he was our new driver and normally we'd have thought no more of it, but this guy was dressed all in white, including his crash helmet, which he never took off. At first we thought it was some sort of anti-nuke blast suit but then we realised he was some sort of racing driver. Actually, we realised that the first time we went out in a car with him. My God, he could make those G-Wagens do things you wouldn't believe. And it's a bloody good job he could drive because the rest of his behaviour was downright weird. He never spoke, he never ate with the rest of us, he used to disappear and then re-appear without explanation. In the early days we used to think he was a Soviet spy but, truth is, the best way to spy is to blend in and this guy, he did the exact opposite. He stood out like a sore thumb. But when things were getting tasty, he always had your back. Always. And for some reason – I can't remember why – we used to call him "Stig". Have you no' got any more of those shortbreads ...?'

Bob could provide me with no explanation of how The Stig had ended up in East Germany any more than I could provide him with some more shortbread. He could, however, give me a brief example of the silent man in white showing his talents during his BRIXMIS days.

'One night we're out at a place called Rangsdorf. Massive Soviet airbase, mostly helicopters, but also the boneyard for crashed aircraft of all sorts. If a MIG went down in East Germany, chances were the wreckage would end up at Rangsdorf. And that made it good for us 'cos we could get in there and have a poke around the guts of a busted Soviet fighter jet. All good intelligence. We'd make our way in at dawn on the basis that Boris would've got pished that night and he'd be fast asleep, even if he was meant to be on guard. Speed was everything. Get in there, have a root around, take a few snaps, few measurements, note anything of interest, get the hell out. Only this time, the Russians must have had their vodka rations cut 'cos it's only just getting light and we've barely had two seconds to poke about when there's a bloody jeep racing towards us and a truck after that, packed with guards. There's just me and my commanding officer and what looks like a hundred angry Ruskies coming for us. If they catch us, we've got a major incident on our hands so, of course, we leg it as fast as we can, heading back to the hole in the fence we came through in the first place. We make it to the fence okay and we're through into the woods on the other side but then we can hear dogs barking in the distance and we know they've got a security unit on the outside, too. They're really not mucking about here. We keep running through the trees and then stop to get our bearings. It's a good two clicks back to where we left Stig and the car and the last thing we want to do on the way is run into a bunch of dogs and angry Commies with guns. So we take a second to figure out our route and we're off again, moving slowly, listening for those dogs getting closer, and it's dark under the trees, which doesn't help much. All of a sudden we hear branches breaking, Russian voices and we start running but now we can hear more barking and I just remember thinking, "This is it, the buggers have got us at last" and then, from nowhere, there's this massive noise, like a roar mixed with smashing – the smashing of branches and small trees – and this bloody great G-Wagen just clatters right through some bushes and slides to a stop in front of us. It's Stig!'

I was going to offer to put the kettle on again but Bob's story was too gripping to interrupt.

'Me and the CO jump in and Stig guns it through the trees,' Bob continued. 'I don't know how he did it as the gaps didnae seem big enough, but we're going at what feels like 200 m.p.h. through those woods, right past one of the Soviet dog patrols and then we're out onto the road, but even then we're not safe 'cos as Stiggy swings the G-Wagen round and points it in the direction of home there's an unmarked car – an old Wartburg I think – parked up just down the road and as we pass 'em they start chasing us. It's our old friends at the Stasi. They're the real bastards, and you didnae want to get caught by them, let me tell you that. But with Stig at the wheel, they didnae stand a chance. We're flying down these lanes through the woods and Stig doesn't even look bothered – it's like he's out for a drive in the country. I saw 'em behind us a couple of times but they were dropping back and back and eventually they were gone and we were back at our base. Stig had saved our skin.'

It was an amazing story and I was keen to know how long The Stig worked in the shadowy world of East German intelligence-gathering. Bob quickly remembers the last time he saw him and it makes for another surprising tale.

'So it's 1989, right. Stig's been working with us for over a year now. Sometimes he'd disappear for a bit but then he'd be back on duty, still driving like a demon. But things are changing out there. It feels like the people are ready for a change, I s'pose. Of course, the authorities don't want that and they're making allowances, letting people travel to the West more freely and so on, but they don't want to lose their power – it's not like they're going to knock down the Berlin Wall or anything. Even so, we're up in East Berlin one night in November and the crowds are gathering as there's some rumour that the gates are going to be opened to allow people into the west of the city. We're hanging about up there, watching what's going on and the answer is, not much. Just a lot of frustrated East Germans and no action.'

A fascinating history lesson, but was this strictly relevant to The Stig? It turns out that it was.

'Old Stiggy, he's not known for his patience. Gets a bit sulky or twitchy if he's bored – usually just wanders off or revs an engine or starts throwing rocks at geese,' Bob observed. 'So we're standing next to the G-Wagen and he's inside it, behind the wheel. Before we know what's happening, he's fired it up and he's off, driving towards the bloody Wall! People are scattering left, right and centre and he's just driving slowly through until he gets to the Wall itself and he just smacks right into it, slow enough not to screw up the Merc, but fast enough to make this massive section of concrete break free. Well, the crowd goes nuts, totally crazy, and they all join in, pushing this slab, trying to make it fall, which eventually it does. And that was basically the last time I saw Stig. Bringing down the Berlin Wall. Then that wee jobby David Hasselhoff turned up and ruined everything.'

Bob could tell me no more but, frankly, I had heard enough. I could deduce no political angle, no particular burning principle behind the actions in these stories. It seemed to me that Stig, if it was indeed *The* Stig, had brought about one of the major political changes of the late twentieth century simply because he was bored.

I thanked Bob for his time and saw him to the door of the hotel room. It was only after he'd gone I noticed that he had taken the flex from the mini kettle. I hoped he didn't use it to strangle someone.

23

DID THE STIG KILL JOHN F. KENNEDY?

No. Of course he didn't. That would be ridiculous. I do wish the publisher hadn't insisted I include this chapter in the contents.

24

THE SURREY FACTOR

As I looked back over my notes so far, I tried to find a recurring theme that tied together all that I had learnt and which might allow me some insight into the enigma of The Stig. At first nothing stood out, but then I alighted upon a geographical commonality that I cursed myself for failing to spot earlier and which all at once seemed so obvious – Surrey.

Almost everyone I had spoken to, every story I had heard, every place I had visited had in some way related to this county. The *Top Gear* test track was there, too, and that was surely as close to a natural home as The Stig had. What was it that connected my subject with the area described by Surrey Chamber of Commerce as 'one of the most successful and productive areas for business in the UK', and by Jeremy Clarkson as 'the patio of England'?

As I wondered how best to find out more about the county and its people, I discovered an organisation which claimed to offer 'The world's only tour of Surrey' and telephoned the number on their rather confusing website. I spoke to a man called Ian who sounded surprised to receive my call, as well as rather distracted, disinterested and ultimately rather annoyed. Nevertheless, he agreed to book me onto a tour leaving at 10.30 a.m. the following Tuesday.

As agreed, I was at Tolworth Station on the south-western fringes of London by half past ten on the agreed date. I waited a good 20 minutes for the promised 'luxury tour bus' to arrive, giving me plenty of time to admire the station car park's chief features, which were a small Indian takeaway (closed) and some cars (parked).

Finally, at just after 10.50 a.m., a faded blue Leyland Sherpa minibus rumbled into the car park bearing the legend 'SURREY TOURS' down both sides, although on the passenger side the word 'Surrey' had been misspelt. The van squeaked noisily to a halt and a tall, wiry, bearded man in safari shorts and a wind-cheater leapt from behind the wheel. 'Are you Mr Doomarseday?' he asked. I corrected his pronunciation of my surname and confirmed that yes, I was the man who had booked 'The Surrey Experience'. He introduced himself as Ian Lentle and apologised for being early, which was either a crude attempt at psychological subterfuge or genuine ineptitude on his part.

I did not acknowledge his remark either way and instead asked if there would be other people joining us on the tour. Lentle snorted derisively. 'No!' he said, loudly. 'Come on, get in the bus,' and with that he slid open the Sherpa's rear door and invited me to step into its damp and strangely fragranced interior. I sat down in the first row of seats in the rear compartment, affording me a ringside view of the subsequent ten-minute pantomime involving Lentle and the sliding door mechanism of his own van, which steadfastly refused to unlatch from the open position. 'Bloody hell!' he cursed several times under his breath as he tugged at it. Still the door would not close. 'Right!' Lentle eventually exclaimed, 'You'll have to help me!' and with that he beckoned me from the van and ordered me to assist him in applying an upward pressure to the entire door until, finally, with a muffled twang, the door came free from its latch and slid noisily into the closed position. 'That's got it!' said Lentle, triumphantly. I suggested that I should sit in the front passenger seat of the van to avoid use of the recalcitrant door, a remark that elicited a needlessly exasperated reaction from Mr Lentle: 'You can't sit there,' he spluttered. 'That's where the buffet car lives.' I peered through the passenger window and noticed that the seat was occupied by a large, blue cool-box. I presumed this was what he meant.

Since Lentle already appeared to be disproportionately enraged by the whole situation, I very cautiously pointed out that I would need to get into the minibus in some way and preferably quite soon, as it was now beginning to drizzle. 'Fine!' he spat, as if enormously inconvenienced by anyone daring to take him up on his crudely advertised services. 'I'll open the door a little bit and you'll have to slide in through the gap.' This would have been fine, but the gap initially proposed by Lentle would have proved challenging for a cat, never mind a fully grown human man. 'I can't risk engaging the catch!' he snapped, when I insisted it was impossible for me to insert myself through the 4-inch slot between the bodywork and the leading edge of the door. Eventually, Lentle relented and slid the door backwards a sufficient distance to permit my graceless ingress, whilst avoiding the troubling grasp of the obstinate catch.

'Right then,' Lentle said, upon rounding the front of the vehicle and clambering behind the steering wheel. 'Let's get this show on the road … OH, FOR GOD'S SAKE …'

Some 15 minutes later, Lentle closed the bonnet, jumped back into the driver's seat and, with a simultaneous jiggling and twisting of the key, coaxed the ageing Leyland's diesel engine into noisy action. We then sat for a further two or three minutes whilst my 'tour guide' struggled to fit a large rubber band around his head, slid a hand-held microphone underneath it and then positioned this device so that it was placed to capture sounds emerging from his mouth. Having completed this fiddly routine, Lentle reached for a box on the dashboard into which the microphone's cable was plugged and flicked a small switch, causing a piercing squall of feedback to echo around the sparse interior of the minibus.

'Okay!' Lentil barked. His single utterance cannoned from the six speakers mounted around the interior above the rear windows at ear-splitting volume. I leaned forward to ask if the PA system might be turned down, but between the noise of the engine and the rubber band now covering much of Lentle's left ear I could not be heard; besides which, my guide was now attempting to effect a U-turn in the car park and, judging from the heavy breathing and noisy grunting being transmitted over the speakers, I thought it best not to distract him from the exertion of manipulating the Sherpa's clearly heavy steering.

'Blast!' he exclaimed at an amplified volume that caused me to clamp my hands over my ears. The U-turn had failed and he was forced to engage reverse, accompanied by a troublesome grinding sound. The van surged backwards with unexpected vigour and there was a dull thud from behind us just as it stopped. 'I think we might have hit something!' I shouted, but it was too late. With a slight increase in the volume of the engine's oily grumblings we were moving forwards again, stopping shortly afterwards at the edge of the station car park as Lentle waited to pull out onto the road. In the relative calm of being stationary I could still hear Lentle's heightened breathing over the speakers, along with a noise that may have been static but seemed more likely to be the sound of his straggly grey beard rubbing against the microphone.

I used the moment to attract Lentle's attention and asked him to turn down the PA system. 'What?' he barked, causing a wild flurry of angry distortion over the speakers in the rear of the minibus. I repeated my request to which Lentle gave a needlessly over-amplified 'tut' but then reached mercifully for the volume knob.

We pulled out of the station car park and headed up a two-lane road towards a large roundabout. 'Ladies and gentlemen,'

Lentle said suddenly and, frankly, unnecessarily. 'Welcome to The Surrey Experience ... OH, COME ON ...' His welcome had been derailed by a dithering motorist ahead who had failed to make use of a gap in traffic to enter the roundabout, and had now become the focus of his ire.

Eventually, the flow of cars ceased for sufficient time to allow the rather slow-moving minibus to lumber noisily onto the roundabout and take the first exit down a slip road onto a faster-moving dual carriageway. The speaker system, which was still uncomfortably loud, allowed me to hear all too clearly the various sounds that were emerging from Lentle's mouth: largely sighs and swear words, although there was at least some half-formed mutterings concerning 'the SODDING gearbox'. Once onto the dual carriageway, we continued, noisily, and with at least one rather odd knocking noise, for perhaps 2 miles until we passed a sign that marked the upper boundary of the county of Surrey. I thought that Lentle might have acknowledged this but he seemed to be busy rummaging around under his seat. Some moments later, he held a small tape machine in front of the microphone strapped to his face and pressed the play button, causing an almost unrecognisably distorted version of the theme from *2001: A Space Odyssey* to burst forth from the speakers – one of which then fell off its bracket and dangled hopelessly from a thin cable.

'Ladies and gentlemen,' Lentle boomed in a strange voice that was presumably meant to sound dramatic. 'We are now entering ... SURREY!'

I refrained from pointing out that we had entered Surrey some three or four minutes before and instead concentrated on moving one row back and to the middle of the minibus in order that I might be as far away as possible from any of the speakers. Happily, Lentle did not notice my discreet movements since he had now engaged on the opening part of what he had entitled 'A Brief History Of Surrey.'

'The first reference to what we now know as Surrey is from the time of King John,' he began. We were now on a motorway section of what I later learned to be the A3. The noise inside the minibus at speed was both enormous and mechanically disturbing, though Lentle's words were remarkably audible since the speaker system was still turned up to an uncomfortably high volume. 'It is referenced in documents from the time as "verily fertile grazing land and most luxurious of aspect", something that I'm sure you'll agree continues to this day!'

Lentle ended this sentence in what he must have considered to be a jocular tone, though his efforts failed since this remark was not remotely amusing, added to which it was almost impossible to see any of Surrey since it was now raining heavily and the minibus windows were steaming up at an alarming rate.

'Ruddy thing!' exclaimed Lentle, rubbing the inside of the windscreen with the sleeve of his jacket whilst, on the outside, a pair of arthritically slow-moving wipers struggled in vain to clear the intense downpour.

'The name Surrey is thought to originate from ancient times,' he continued. 'It derives from the Chinese "Soo-Ree" which means "bountiful land near London" and was the name given by merchants from the Orient who came here to buy wood such as oak and willow and other woods, which were grown in plentiful numbers across the county.'

I had read a few things about the history of Surrey since booking this tour and, whilst I would not describe myself as an expert, I was almost certain that this was incorrect. However, since I was effectively a prisoner in his deafening and uncomfortably pitching minibus as we clattered down the A3, I decided it was pointless to engage with Lentle unless the smell of diesel got any stronger.

'The modern use of the name Surrey most likely dates from Tudor times, when it became a popular holiday destination for wealthy Londonites and also for royalty such as Kings Henry the Eighth, Edward the Fifth and the other ones. They would use Surrey's rolling lands and thick woods to hunt animals such as boar, wolf and bear, all of which lived here in those times, one thousand years ago.'

By now I was certain that Lentle's crackly lecture was complete drivel. I just hoped that his information about modern Surrey was more accurate than both his history and his ability to steer a minibus.

After what felt like several hours of extreme engine noise and some utter rubbish about 'the British civil war against Sweden', Lentle jerked the ageing Sherpa onto a slip road and announced with needless grandeur and volume that we were now approaching 'the ancient town or city of Guildford'.

'Flakey Jesus!' he added, rather unexpectedly. It quickly transpired that this exclamation was brought on by failure to take a right turn that was, itself, brought on by Lentle's almost total lack of forward visibility due to the heavy condensation still covering most of the windscreen.

He elected to effect an immediate U-turn in front of a church, even though we appeared to be on a major thoroughfare and the minibus was plainly rather slow and arduous to manoeuvre in such situations. Sure enough, the process took far longer than was comfortable, elicited a large amount of unpleasantly amplified exertion from the driver, and inconvenienced a significant number of other motorists, one of whom persuaded Lentle to wind down his window just as the turn was completed in order that she might call him a 'stupid old git'.

'I'm 53,' Lentle replied ineffectually as we lurched forwards, accompanied by the familiar crunch of gears and the less familiar smell of something becoming dangerously hot.

As we stopped at some traffic lights on the outskirts of the town I could take no more and crept forward through the passenger compartment to address Lentle directly. I insisted that it would be beneficial to both of us if the PA system was switched off and I came to sit in the front passenger seat. 'I've told you,' Lentle replied, peevishly. 'The canteen occupies that seat. I can't move it because I might need access to it to serve you an in-flight snack. Now, for safety reasons, please take your seat.'

'I don't want anything from the canteen,' I shouted as the minibus lurched forwards once more and I stumbled back to my place in the second row of rear seats. Barely had I sat down again when, without warning, a can of Panda Cola and a Mars bar came flying towards me from the front of the vehicle, both narrowly missing my head. I picked up these items from the floor to discover that they were both extremely wet and that the chocolate was dated 'Best before September 2003'.

'The name Guildford comes from Roman times,' Lentle continued, signally failing to acknowledge that he had just thrown snacks at my face. 'It means "guilty ford" and indicates that in historic times there was a river crossing where those who committed crimes or infidelities would be taken to be beaten with reeds.'

I have subsequently checked this information and it is not even remotely true.

The minibus roared onto a multi-lane one-way system and we began circling a central area, repeatedly driving round and round the same loop of road with ever increasing pointlessness. The noise, smell and dampness inside the creaking Sherpa was becoming unbearable and Lentle's obnoxiously loud commentary became no more acquainted with the truth as he droned on about 'the Scottish conquests in the search for yeast' or some such nonsense.

All I could do to close my eyes and hope this frightful endeavour would end, until eventually I was distracted by the vibration of my mobile phone. It was Les Dennis, no doubt calling for a friendly chat about sales of our recent work, *Les-ing Up*. With regret I had to reject his call since it would have been almost impossible to hear him, even though I know from experience that Les has excellent projection.

'Right,' Lentle said loudly from the front seat as we veered without warning off the one-way system and down a two-lane road that led out of town. 'That concludes Guildford. To Woking!'

Thankfully, at this point we stopped at a red light and I was able to scuttle forward to address Lentle again. 'Mr Lentle,' I said. 'I must insist that you stop for a moment.'

'Jesus!' Lentle exclaimed in an exasperated tone. Nonetheless, when the light turned green we lurched forwards, across a roundabout and then swung violently into a petrol station on the left. I fumbled for the handle to release me from my humid prison and, without thinking, slid the door all the way back to permit my escape. 'Oh, for God's sake!' Lentle cried as he rounded the front of the minibus. 'You bloody idiot, now we'll have to get it off the damn catch again. This is putting us completely behind schedule.'

I was rather surprised by this last remark and asked what schedule he was referring to.

'There's a tight schedule for this tour,' Lentle exclaimed, as if this was a ludicrous question. 'I don't just make it up as I go along, you know.'

I was about to suggest that this was precisely what he appeared to be doing but thought better of it and decided instead to stop wasting my time and his by cutting straight to the chase. I explained that I was working on a biography of The

Stig, that Surrey seemed to feature heavily in his backstory and that I wondered if there was anything that could link the county to the make-up of the man.

'I have no idea what you're talking about,' Lentle huffed. 'Now please help me release the door so we can get going again.'

I stated firmly that I was not ready to get back in the van and implored him to think harder about how Surrey might have had a unique effect on a mute speed demon.

'Look, you're putting us extremely behind,' Lentle grumbled. 'If we don't get moving right now I'm going to have to start the Woking section of the tour right here.' He gestured towards a large metallic box nearby and pulled a face, as if to suggest that rampantly inaccurate drivel about local history could not be dispensed within 6 feet of a tyre inflation machine.

Secretly, I was wondering if the Woking segment would be more pure fiction or if the bearded lunatic had taken time to read my acclaimed work on the town's most famous son, *Paul Weller: Mod To Misery-guts*. However, I kept this to myself and reiterated that I had no intention of setting foot inside the minibus again until I had taken more lungfuls of air that weren't almost tangibly wet with diesel fumes.

'Fine,' Lentle spat. He drew breath and then began speaking in an insanely strident manner. 'Woking was founded by the Elizabethans who believed the land upon which it stood was blessed by the gods of succulent vegetables …'

I implored Lentle to stop this madness but he continued unabated with some utter nonsense about earthquakes, until eventually I could take no more and simply walked off. It felt rather good to do so and I wondered if this was how The Stig felt when he simply walked away from situations that bored or displeased him, as was his habit.

As I reached the edge of the petrol station and turned right onto the pavement, I heard Lentle's voice calling after me.

'Where on earth are you going?' he shouted, brusquely.

I stopped and walked a little way back towards the shorts-wearing madman and his ludicrous 'tour bus', before telling him that I was going home.

Lentle looked genuinely confused, as well as typically annoyed. I realised he still had the large rubber band strapped around his head. 'What?' he spluttered. 'Why?'

'Mr Lentle,' I said, firmly. 'Your tour is terrible.'

With that, I turned smartly and headed in the general direction of the town centre.

'Well, at least I'm not wearing trousers,' Lentle shouted after me, confusingly.

I found Guildford railway station and caught a train back to London. During the journey I began to worry that Lentle's tour had been so uselessly uninformative that it had actually pushed existing information about Surrey out of my head. Worse than that, it had got me no closer to understanding why The Stig seemed so closely aligned to this county. With no concrete evidence to go on, I started to accept that perhaps it was just a coincidence.

25

LOST IN SHOWBIZ

The farcical tour of Surrey in a crap van had been a waste of time and I was becoming concerned that I had taken off on too much of a random tangent in my efforts to find the real Stig. I needed to get back to basics and think again about the role that made him famous in the first place – as *Top Gear's* tame racing driver.

I had watched him at work and enjoyed seeing the effortless skill with which he took cars to the absolute upper edge of their performance envelope. I had also noted the calm, silent ease with which he appeared to coach a celebrity guest in the Reasonably Priced Car. This latter aspect intrigued me. If you look at the list of the famous people who have appeared on *Top Gear*, you realise that The Stig has met a remarkable and glittering cavalcade of stars; unlike James May who confessed to me that he often missed saying hello to the guests because the time they had to hang around backstage often coincided with his 'gentleman's quality lavatory time'.

What struck me about watching The Stig working with a star guest, as I had done with Matt Smith, was how seemingly unaffected he was in the presence of a celebrity. I rang Jeremy Clarkson, the other person who spends time with the guests on *Top Gear*, to find out more.

'Have you got the American military to admit to the super-soldier project yet?' the presenter barked down the line. I lied and said the Pentagon was considering my request before hurriedly changing the subject by asking if The Stig really was utterly impervious to star quality.

'You'd think so,' Clarkson shouted. 'But it's not quite as simple as all that. In the beginning, yes, he didn't seem to give a toss either way. It's not like he was constantly hanging around, shoving bits of paper under people's noses so he could get an autograph. Apart from with Michael Gambon – never did get to the bottom of that one. But then it all changed ... Look, I'm going to have to ring you back, there's a *really* strong smell of burning coming from somewhere ...'

Happily, that same day I was exchanging e-mails with former *Top Gear* associate producer, Helen Duvet, and she was able to shed some light on what Clarkson had alluded to.

'The turning point for The Stig and celebs was when we sent him to the National Television Awards in 2008,' she wrote. 'Jeremy, Richard and James couldn't go because they were in studio for the new series. We thought it would be funny to get Stig to go instead! Don't know if he understood what was going on but he played along for once and got in the limo to take him to the awards without making a fuss. We gave him a letter from our presenters to be read out if we won. As a finishing touch, we put a bow tie and a silk scarf on him. It was worth it, even though seven people got injured in the process!'

What surprised the *Top Gear* team was how much The Stig enjoyed the awards show, as Duvet went on to explain in her e-mail.

'We won the award and (with a bit of a prod in the back!) Stig went up to collect it. It all worked very well. Very funny telly! Once the award had been presented, the plan was for someone to grab Stig backstage and get him out of there as soon as possible. The problem was, no-one could find him! He'd disappeared completely! Shocker! Eventually someone found him at the after-show party. He was hanging out with Dannii Minogue, Denise van Outen, Phil Schofield etc. etc. When we heard, everyone in the TG office was really shocked! It was so unlike him.'

Was it possible The Stig had been genuinely affected by the glamorous world of the celebrity party? Happily, later that afternoon, Jeremy Clarkson finally called me back.

'Sorry about that. I found the cause of the burning smell,' he shouted down the phone. 'The cause turned out to be a fire. It's out now and I've bought a new microwave so everything is under control.'

I told him I had heard about the 2008 National Television Awards and wondered if this was a pivotal moment in The Stig's relationship with celebrities.

'No doubt at all – that was the moment when it all went wrong,' he agreed. 'I mean, up until that point The Stig might have had a few celebs he hung about with sometimes. Chris Packham, Cheggers, Lemmy out of Motörhead, that crowd. But after the NTAs everything was different. Suddenly he'd gone all ITV. He was papped having coffee with Amanda Holden or coming out of a shop with Myleene Klass. He was in *Heat* magazine literally every single week.'

Clarkson went on to reveal that The Stig was hanging out with the light entertainment A-list even when there wasn't a photographer lurking nearby.

'I once went round to Simon Cowell's house to borrow his strimmer and Stig was just there, sitting on the sofa,' the presenter thunders. 'Although it was actually quite hard to see him because everything in Cowell's place is white.'

According to Clarkson, The Stig's new showbiz lifestyle started to impact on his 'day job' as *Top Gear's* tame racing driver.

'I don't know what he was playing at, but it became literally impossible to track him down when you needed him, probably because he was horse riding with Cheryl Cole or going to Laser Quest with Ant and/or Dec.'

The worst, however, was yet to come, as Clarkson explained: 'It's one thing to be late to the studio because you've been at the cinema with Tess Daly or having a picnic with Ken Barlow out of Take That, but then he started hanging around with celebrities at night and that's when we completely lost control of him. Imagine Lindsay Lohan times a hundred. It was literally Lohundred. He was constantly being spotted coming out of nightclubs with some girls from *EastEnders* or a Girl Aloud or something, and it just got worse and worse. He seemed to be out all night sometimes and, of course, that just made him more of a target for the paparazzi. Imagine Lindsay Lohan times a thousand. It was literally Lohthousand.'

The Stig's legendary speed only made things worse, according to Clarkson.

'It was bad enough that he was becoming notorious all over London,' the presenter explains. 'But then we started hearing that he'd been clubbing with the cast of *Hollyoaks* in Manchester and at a bar with some people off *X Factor* in London *on the same night*. Imagine Lindsay Lohan times a million. It was Lohmillion ... sorry, I'm not sure these are working. Forget I said that. The point is, The Stig was out of control.'

Curiously, there is no evidence to suggest that The Stig was doing anything reckless or illegal. He has never been seen drinking and all *Top Gear* staff past and present agree that he probably doesn't touch alcohol or any other intoxicants. Yet his constant presence on the celebrity party scene was still a cause for concern amongst the programme's producers, not least because it seemed so at odds with the cool and mysterious image he projected on television.

'We worked damn hard to keep him out of the papers,' Clarkson recalls. 'But he was just becoming ridiculous. Worse than that, The Stig had lost sight of who he was.'

I was just asking Clarkson to expand on this point when there was a loud expletive and a muffled bang down the line.

'I have to go,' he barked. 'You should contact Jay Kay out of Jamiroquai. Ask him about the party at his place. You'll get the idea. I really have to go. There's a lot of smoke coming from what I think is called the "washing machine" ...'

As luck would have it, I had a number for Jay Kay out of Jamiroquai's assistant and she quickly returned my call to say that the singer would be happy to talk about the party Clarkson had alluded to. Just two days later, I was piloting my rented car up the driveway of his rambling mansion in the countryside.

I stepped from my hired Toyota and took a moment to admire the weathered elegance of this vast pile. It was quite the fitting home for a multi-platinum-selling artist. I hopped up the front step and swung the hefty metal knocker firmly against its worn black base. Almost immediately the vast oak door swung open and Jay Kay out of Jamiroquai's housekeeper greeted me.

'Mr Papier-Mâché?' she said, slightly incorrectly. 'Mr Kay out of Jamiroquai is expecting you,' she continued, beckoning me into the vast entrance hall. 'He's in the sitting room. It's that door there ...' With that she pointed me to a plain wooden door on the left-hand side of the hallway and indicated for me to open it.

As I did, a voice from inside spoke: 'Hey!' it said. 'Welcome! Welcome! Are you Simon?' There, standing in the middle of the room, was Jay Kay out of Jamiroquai himself. He was elegantly dressed in black trousers and a well-cut black shirt, topped off with a rather outlandish hat that appeared to be made of fur. The room itself was decorated in a classical yet modern style with many items of furniture seemingly arranged at random. The singer gave me a firm handshake and invited me to sit down on the black leather sofa. He remained standing as he spoke once more.

'So, old Jezza told you about the party with The Stig?' he said, grinning impishly. I was about to confirm that he had and ask for more details when I became aware that the sofa was moving sideways towards the end of the room. Kay must have sensed my disquiet. 'Don't worry, it does that,' he said, expertly performing a small but quite funky dance-move to get out of the way of an armchair that had also begun to move briskly across the room.

'So, yeah, the famous party,' the unusually hatted singer continued. 'I mean, I make no secret of it. I like a party as much as the next man, but this was just crazy, it really was.' As he finished this sentence, he hopped effortlessly onto the arm of another sofa that was now trundling vertically across the room. My own sofa was now moving at quite low speed back towards the centre of the room. As I silently prayed that it would stop, I invited Kay to explain to me what made this party so particularly noteworthy.

'I'd met Stig before at *Top Gear* and always thought he was a good bloke and all that,' the popular funkster explained, hopping lightly down from the silently shifting sofa and dodging around a small desk that was moving purposefully towards the back wall. 'So when he turned up here unexpectedly one night, I was pretty happy about that. I'd heard he was going a bit nuts for the partying but, hey, there's no shame in going a bit crazy once in a while so I said, "Great! Let's have a party right here in my gaff." I got the tunes pumping, made a few calls to get some other people over and we were in business.'

The housekeeper entered the room with a tray bearing a pot of tea and two mugs which, with some skill, she placed onto the coffee table as it moved steadily across the room. Kay watched her put it down, thanked her and then continued with his tale.

'So, pretty soon we've got a right crowd of nutters in the place,' he remembers. 'You know the people – Moira Stewart, Aled Jones, Ken Bruce off Radio 2, most of the people from *Country-file*. Party animals, basically. The whole place is jumping. And then BBC News's business editor Robert Peston turns up. Well, when The Pest is in the house, you know you've got a party, right?'

The diminutive vocalist performed an elegant spin and side-ways hop on the spot to avoid an approaching occasional table and shimmied across the room to pour the tea. As he did so, the coffee table, which had been static for a few seconds, suddenly started sliding across the floor, causing Kay to spill the tea. 'Every bloody time,' he muttered, before being forced to roll out of the way as a low bookcase sped across the room and almost mowed him down. While he picked himself up, my constantly shifting seat happened to roll backwards past the singer and, as I slid by, I offered to help with the dispensing of the hot drinks.

'No! Stay there!' Kay barked urgently. 'Sorry, but just stay put,' he said more calmly. 'It's just safer if you stay on the sofa and ...' His words were cut short as he was forced to leap sideways to avoid a console table that was moving at some speed towards the front of the room.

'I'll come back to the tea,' Kay said. 'First, let me tell you about this party.' He performed a stylish 180-degree spin and fell perfectly into a low leather armchair as it rolled past.

'So, this place is really going wild, right. We've got the music on loud, we've got booze, we've got celebrities, and there, in the middle of it all, is The Stig. And, believe me, he's loving it. I mean, he ain't drinking or dancing or doing anything, really, but he's loving it. He's loving this non-stop party. Then, after 24 hours or so, people are dropping left, right and centre. I remember, John Craven came up to me and said, "Jay, I'm going to have to call it a day," and that never normally happens. You know what they say – the party's over when Craven ain't ravin'. Trouble is, the party isn't over. Stig won't let it end. I'm feeling pretty knackered myself but he just won't let me stop. I'm having to call more people to keep things going. I've got mopeds arriving with more pizzas, I've got BBC2 arts presenter Mark Lawson freestyling over some pretty savage tunes; I've got Huw Edwards and Kirsty Wark in a cab on their way, promising to keep the vibe going … It's mental, man, just mental. I've never had a party like it, and The Stig just won't quit.'

As my sofa reversed into the wall and then began sliding sideways towards the window, Kay's armchair stopped moving around the room for a moment and he took the opportunity to stand up, hopping out of the way of an antique bureau that was trundling towards him.

'Eventually, after like three days of solid partying, I've run out of booze, I've run out of tunes and I've run out of party-mad celebs I can call to keep this thing going. I remember, I showed Peter Cockroft the weather man to the door and then I said to Stig, "Look, mate, I think that's it, this party is over."'

Kay twirled on one foot to avoid a fast moving nest of tables and fell over the back of a sofa that was sliding rapidly across the floor.

'Oh for God's sake …' the singer cursed, expertly rolling backwards and landing on his feet, just avoiding been run over by a fast-paced wingback chair. He vaulted over one of its low arms and sat down.

'Well, that's when things went mad,' Kay continued. 'Stig went nuts, like proper, loony nuts. He's throwing leftover pizza about the place, he's smashing open gold discs and lobbing them like Frisbees. I go into the kitchen and find he's smashed up a saxophone then put it into the microwave, set it to cook for 70 hours and then disappeared. Suddenly, from outside, I hear this engine noise. Oh my God! He's got into my garage! My beautiful cars! I leg it out there just in time to see my Lamborghini Miura, my gorgeous Miura SV, flying across the lawn and, splash! straight into the swimming pool. I run over and just as I get there, Stig pops to the surface and climbs out of the water. I was pissed off, man, so pissed off. I like a party, I really do, but this was insane. And it was The Stig. He's not meant to do stuff like that. I knew at that point he'd gone too far. He'd lost his respect for cars.'

As my slowly moving sofa mercifully stopped for a moment, I suddenly knew what Jeremy Clarkson had meant when he said The Stig had lost sight of who he was. All the partying was one thing, but when one of the world's greatest drivers loses his appreciation of cars, it must have been clear that this situation was serious. I stood up and went to shake Jay Kay's hand. He, too, attempted to stand but as he did, the wingback began to move forwards and he was tipped into an unfortunate stumble.

'Jesus! I've had 16 years of this crap,' he cursed under his breath. 'I'm so sorry mate, a man was supposed to be coming to look at this again ...' He gestured to the room full of randomly arranged furniture, much of which was still moving inexplicably across or down the floor space.

Kay showed me out of the house and cheerily wished me well with my writing endeavours. As I went to get into my car I looked up and saw the singer still smiling at me, and waving as he started to close the door. Behind him I noticed a large bookcase was moving rapidly towards him and I tried to call out to warn him. All too late, the door closed and a second later there was a dull thump from within.

Upon my return to London, I called Jeremy Clarkson to tell him that my chat with Jay Kay had been most enlightening and that I now realised that if The Stig had lost his respect for cars, the situation must have become truly critical.

'Good man,' Clarkson coughed down the line. 'You can see the problem we had now. It was insane, and pretty soon the press was going to be all over it.

The only way to control it was to distract them with another *Top Gear* story. I had to keep sparking fury just to keep The Stig away from the front pages. It was exhausting. In the end, it just wasn't enough. We had to go to DEFCON 1 …'

What, I asked, did that entail?

'I can't explain now,' he barked. 'This toom-ball dry-har machine is making a very strange noise and I'm not sure it's cooking my pork chops at all. Call our old producer, Rob – he's the one to tell you. OH MY GOD …'

I left Clarkson to his domestic appliance concerns and duly made contact with *Top Gear*'s senior producer from the time. Little could I have guessed that what he was about to tell me was truly extraordinary …

26

THE BEN COLLINS INCIDENT

Another domestic appliance-related mishap had prevented Jeremy Clarkson from telling me what *Top Gear* did to counter The Stig's wildly partying lifestyle and loss of respect for his most beloved objects, but I was able to contact former senior producer Rob Tongue to find out more.

Tongue, a friendly man with a shock of red hair and a confusingly fashionable T-shirt, agrees to meet me in a pub called The Smashed Crab near Chertsey.

'Oh, yeah, what we came to call Operation Rumpole,' the producer says, wiping a drip of condensation from the side of his beer glass. 'What you've got to realise is, we needed a drastic measure. The Stig's constant celebrity partying was way out of control and everyone was worried, not just at *Top Gear* but at the very highest level within the BBC. I remember, we had a lot of meetings about it. A *lot* of meetings. It's often the way, and these meetings gave us a chance to talk through all of our options. If memory serves, at one of the meetings someone in

Beeb management asked why we couldn't just give The Stig "a good talking to". All of us lot from the *Top Gear* side had a good laugh at that one. Yeah, right. As if he's going to listen to that, right? Another suggestion was that we sack him. Like I said, we needed drastic action. The trouble was, The Stig was a major part of the show and we really didn't want to get rid of him. Besides, we got the contracts department to look into it and it turned out that technically we didn't employ him in the first place. He'd been on the show for more than six years and we weren't bloody paying him! We kept him in fast cars and raw mince and he kept showing up. Or, at least, he kept showing up until he got distracted by his celeb mates.'

Tongue says the only thing that everyone in the BBC meetings could eventually agree on was engineering some sort of enormous distraction.

'It had to be big,' Tongue points out, draining his lager. 'Jeremy was doing his best to get himself in the papers and keep The Stig out of them. Trouble was, there were only so many times he could claim the Scottish smell of poo and all Belgians are lesbians or smash through something in a car like an oaf, before the press would get bored. I mean, you couldn't fault him for trying. At one point he got so desperate he jumped into a car and smashed through a brick wall when we weren't even filming. Crazy. Especially since it turned out the car belonged to one of our researchers. She was pretty upset about it. Anyway, to keep attention off The Stig, we needed something much bigger. And believe me, we got it.'

I buy Tongue another pint of beer and he explains that a small team met in secret in the *Top Gear* office to thrash out the details of an audacious distraction that would keep The Stig's partying antics off the front pages.

'It was actually pretty simple,' he says, looking around nervously in case any of our fellow late-afternoon drinkers are listening. 'We would get someone to pretend to be The Stig. They would "out" themselves, claim they'd been him all along and, to really string it out, they would announce they were about to publish a "tell-all" book about it. It was genius. The papers would go nuts for it and, meanwhile, anyone spotting the real Stig coming out of some nightclub would assume it was some nutter in a fancy-dress costume. Done right, it would buy us the time to get Stiggy himself under control. All we needed was someone to stand up and claim they were the man inside the suit. And, as you know, that person was Ben.'

Ben Collins was a professional racing driver who had appeared as himself on *Top Gear* during some of Richard Hammond's amusingly inappropriate vehicle races and car-football matches. As Tongue tells it, he was the ideal candidate to claim he had been The Stig all along.

'Good old Ben was a mate of the show,' Tongue explains. 'And we all agreed he'd do a great job of pretending he was Stig. Truth is, I think he wanted to be like The Stig, anyway. He already owned a white crash helmet and he had a very similar race suit and boots, too. Plus, we'd heard that people at race meetings had started asking him if he was The Stig and he'd always replied, "Might be ...". I think he liked people to assume that he was. It was perfect. He already knew loads about The Stig so it would be no problem for him to go the whole hog and tell the world it was him behind the visor. All he had to do was sit down and write a book about it, and we would pay him to do that using the profits that the Beeb's commercial side had made from the massive success of selling Stig soap-on-a-rope.'

Collins was given just a few weeks to pen his 'revealing' book, but the writing process soon hit trouble.

'Ben started well, but then he began to run out of "anecdotes" about his time as the tame racing driver,' Rob Tongue recalls. 'I remember him phoning me one day fretting that he couldn't think of anything interesting to say about being The Stig any more. I told him it didn't matter; it was just about getting the headlines and he should just stick in some stories from his real life to fill up the pages. He took my advice and bunged in a load of irrelevant stuff about racing and being in the Territorial Army, which did the job a treat.'

The really audacious part of the subterfuge was yet to come, however. *Top Gear* knew that if the book was published without much fanfare its impact would be relatively limited. They had to create a buzz around it by making it seem as if the BBC actively wanted to prevent the book from reaching the shops and that meant only one thing – they would have to take Ben Collins to court.

'We were all a bit nervous about this, but it had to be done,' Tongue remembers, taking a deep swig of his drink. 'I remember Ben getting really antsy, fretting about how much it was going to cost him if it all went wrong. I had to remind him it didn't matter as it wasn't his cash at stake. We were playing the system with our soap-on-a-rope money.'

The Stig court case went ahead exactly as planned, and the newspapers went wild for the story of a humble racing driver who had tired of anonymity and wanted to tell his side of the story. No-one ever guessed that it was all an elaborate ruse. In the end, the courts ruled in Collins's favour and the book was published, but for the *Top Gear* team it didn't matter either way. They had successfully created their distraction.

'The whole plan worked brilliantly,' Tongue said with delight. 'Trouble is, it had really only bought us time. We still needed to sort out The Stig and stop him being such a celeb whore. Now, that wasn't going to be easy because by now Stig is in LA, partly because he's totally lost in showbiz and partly because if he stays in the UK, Jay Kay out of Jamiroquai is going to kill him. Luckily, I knew a bloke out there who specialised in this sort of thing. He's called Paul Trent. Ex-nightclub bouncer from around Dagenham way. Lives out there now, sorting out exactly these sorts of problems. He was just the man for the job.'

Tongue picked up his mobile, jabbed briefly at the screen and then turned it to me so that I could copy down the number displayed under the name 'Trenty'.

'Give him a call,' Tongue said, breezily. 'Tell him I sent you. He'll be able to fill you in on how he did it. How he got The Stig back.'

By that evening I had made contact with Paul Trent, and he quickly agreed to give me the full story behind the return of The Stig.

'I knew this was gonna be a tricky one,' Trent said, his gruff London accent peppered with transatlantic tinges brought on by years of living in the US. 'So, first thing I'm gonna need is some help. And I couldn't have got a better person to help me – Paris Hilton. Now, what a lot of people don't know about Paris is that she's a massive car nerd. Subscribes to all the car magazines, *Road & Track*, *Car & Driver*, you name it. You get stuck in a car with her on a long journey – and believe me I have – you just can't shut her up about differentials and camshafts and all that. So when she finds out that The Stig has gone proper mental and it might stop him from setting fast laps on *Top Gear*, she's pretty upset. "We gotta do something, Pauly, he's the benchmark!" she said to me. "If The Stig can't do the laps, all the existing lap times are rendered irrelevant as a fair comparison between performance cars!" I said, "I know, princess, but we might be able to stop this." Well, she agreed to help me straight away.'

From 5,000 miles down the line, Trent chuckled slightly and then continued his story.

'So, Paris and me, we come up with a plan to trap The Stig,' he explained. 'Well, actually, it was her idea, really. She's a smart girl and don't let no-one tell you otherwise. She says she'll host a fake doggy party at her house and invite The Stig along. See, by this point, The Stig has gone totally frigging Beverly Hills and got himself a little dog – a Chihuahua, I think. Nutter. He's gone totally la-la so he'll definitely accept the invitation and when he shows up to Paris's place, me and my boys will grab him. The invitations go out and the bait is set. Now, to avoid arousing suspicion, Paris really is putting on a party and she's invited the cream of Hollywood small dog enthusiasts. Come the day, they're all there: Jack Nicholson, Bruce Willis, Axl Rose, the lot. And suddenly, there he is. The Stig's fetched up, just as we expected, and he's mincing about by the pool with this bloody mutt under his arm. I remember, we let everyone relax for a bit then Paris looks at me, winks and calls everyone down her massive garden and out into the middle of the lawn where she pulls the sheet off a large crate and announces that she's got an amazing new dog that she wants to show off. So all the guests are crowded round and Stig, he's right at the front, which is just perfect. With a load of ceremony, Paris opens the crate but there ain't a dog inside – it's my boys from the extraction team and they come flying out with massive nets to catch The Stig. Of course, old Stiggy, he ain't going down without a fight and he's a fast little bugger so, straight off, he makes a run for it. I dive through the crowd to grab him but I'm beaten to it by Mickey Rourke, who's got him by the arm and is shouting, "Give in, Stig! This life ain't worth it!" I mean, this Hollywood lot, they're used to these interventions when someone's got problems; it's all pretty normal to them, I guess. Anyway, Stig gives Rourke the slip but by then

Jason Statham has put down his Pekingese and is trying to rugby-tackle Stig to the ground, and Matt Damon is right behind him shouting, "It's okay, Stig. Your people need you!" I'm in hot pursuit as we're running back towards the house and I'm being overtaken by Vin Diesel who's still got his prize Maltese under his arm. So Statham tries for a full-on tackle but hits the deck and Damon falls over him, taking down Diesel in the process. It's bloody carnage. I'm still running and now I've got Russell Crowe with me and he's shouting, "Let it go, Stig!" with his Pomeranian at his heels. Up ahead I see my old mate, Steve Seagal, but Stig just doesn't stop and shoulder-barges him out of the way, sending him flying into some bushes. I look back to make sure he's okay and he's on the ground sobbing with his Shih Tzu licking at his face, but that don't help us to catch The Stig and he's almost at the house now, which is just gonna cause more agro if we don't stop him. Crowe and me are slowing now but Kiefer Sutherland is on a charge, carrying his King Charles in a bag, but I don't think he's gonna catch up. Stig's just getting to the veranda when, from nowhere, this figure steps out from behind a statue and delivers the most almighty karate chop to Stig's collarbone. The poor sod didn't know what's hit him and he goes down like a sack of crap in the face of this incredible assailant. Well, I should have known who it was 'cos it's someone you can always rely on in this kind of situation. It's Meryl Streep. "Cheers, Mezza," I says as I reach her. "No problem, Pauly," she replies, "I just want Stig to go back to doing what he does best." She's a diamond is Meryl. Lovely lady.'

The line goes quiet as Trent pauses for a moment. I prompt him to continue by asking what happened next.

'Well, my boys are on the scene in seconds,' the celebrity security expert explains. 'And they get Stig subdued and then put him into the crate on the lawn. We get that onto a truck and we ship out to a top-secret addiction clinic in Arizona. Bloke who runs it is a guy called Dr Eugene Spaycebatts and he's developed these radical techniques to cure addictions. So, in Stig's case, he breaks his celebrity addiction by strapping him to a chair and showing him paparazzi photos of celebs failing their driving tests or getting into a Toyota Prius or whatever. Basically, he made The Stig associate trashy celebrities with the two things he hates the most: bad driving and boring cars. And it worked like a charm. Two months later, I packed him off to the UK, good as gold. We drove past one of the Kardashian girls on the way to LAX. Stig didn't react at all. That's when I knew he was truly cured.'

After talking to Paul Trent, I rang former producer Rob Tongue to thank him for the contact and to tell him that Trent's story had been most enlightening.

'Amazing, isn't it? And it worked better than we could ever have imagined,' Tongue said. 'Of course, we still had to think of a way of dealing with the whole Ben Collins situation on the show. Publically, we'd sacked him and we needed a new Stig. But then we had this idea to find a "baby Stig" during the Middle East special. When the next series started we came up with some bollocks about how he'd grown into a full-size Stig in a matter of weeks and he was ready to get out on the track, business as usual. At the time I don't think anyone realised there wasn't a new Stig at all. It was the same bloody Stig all along!'

Tongue laughed to himself down the line and I thanked him for his time. 'No worries, mate,' he said. 'Thank God for soap-on-a-rope, eh? It basically saved The Stig.'

27

PIPPA'S BOTTOM

The Stig had been rescued from the darkest corners of show business and successfully cured of his addiction to minor-league celebrities, allowing him to settle down to a gentler existence and to do what he did best out on the test track. That's not to say The Stig completely renounced the celebrity world, because it seems he formed close bonds with certain stars, though they were a quieter, classier bunch than the soap starlets and ex-boy-band members he had once accompanied to exclusive nightclubs across the world. And, as I was about to find out, The Stig became close friends with a person who wasn't well known at all, though she was shortly to become one of the most famous women in the world. Her name was Pippa Middleton.

I discovered this remarkable friendship quite unexpectedly whilst at an evening function to celebrate the launch of Ross Kemp's new range of exfoliating facial scrubs. There, I bumped into a PR professional called Camilla Bergman. I have known

Camilla for a long time, ever since she gave me a very smart, limited-edition jacket from the short-lived 'Jon Snow at Asda' range in return for raiding my contact book in order to bolster the turnout for the party she was organising to commemorate 30 years of Pam Ayres.

In conversation, I mentioned that I was working on a biography of The Stig and immediately she let out a high-pitched screech. 'Oh! My! God!' she exclaimed. 'Stiggy! You're writing about Stiggy! Golly! I know Stig. Well, I don't really *know* him; he's actually a mate of Pips Middleton.'

Camilla is an old school friend of Pippa's and her words immediately piqued my interest. Happily, she invited me to drop by her office the next day where she would give me 'the goss' on this intriguing connection.

'Pips and Stiggy, pretty weird, yeah?' Camilla drawled the following morning, as she leaned forward onto her desk in the airy offices of Cams & Tams PR in Fulham. 'Strictly platonic, of course, but you know they really are BFFs [author's note: according to the internet this means 'best friends forever']. What do they talk about? Probably nothing, right? Because, you know, he doesn't speak, does he? Haaa!'

I was curious to know how The Stig and Ms Middleton had met in the first place, and Camilla seemed to have the answer.

'Quite a while ago now Pips used to work in a shop in Notting Hill that sold dried flowers,' she said, idly twirling her large sunglasses in her hand before replacing them on the top of her head. 'I mean, she basically ran the place if truth be told.

Anyway, one day Stig walks in and wants to buy a massive bundle of dried roses so Pips sells them to him, and then basically after that he was in there every other day – even every day sometimes – buying more and more dried flowers. Heaven alone knows what he was doing with them but, the point is, that's how Pips and Stig became chums. Eventually Pips quits her job in the shop. I mean, it's a brutal world, the dried flower business, and I think she'd had enough, but she kept in touch with a few of her favourite customers and, in particular, with Mr Stiggy. And that's basically the story, right?'

Pippa's friendship with The Stig didn't end there, however, because the so-called tame racing driver was to have a profound effect on her appearance: one that would catapult her into the limelight at her own sister's wedding.

'Right, so Stig has been knocking around with Pips and the gang for a while. We used to see him about all the time then sometimes not for, like, ages, you know. But he and Pips were deffers still mates. So then, fast forward to, like, late 2010, right? Pip's sister Kate is marrying Wills the following April, going to be wedding of the year, totes exciting! And Pips is going to be chief bridesmaid,' Camilla recalls. 'Happy times. But she's a bit worried that she's basically going to be seen by millions of people on telly all around the world wearing this fabulous dress and she's got to get in shape, yeah? Classic problem. So what she does is she basically finds this yoga and nutrition, you know, *guru* round here in Fulham, and then basically she wants the whole gang to go along with her for the first consultation. You know, moral support and all that. So there we all are, me and Ems and Arabella and Stig, trooping into this yoga studio-cum-laboratory place. It was totes hilarious! And this guru chappy, he starts asking her all these questions and it's a bit random, actually, and then he basically starts pointing at her body and asking what shape she wants to be. It's all, like, really embarrassing. And he gets to, you know, her bum and he asks what she wants to do with that. By this point, Ems and Bells and me are just cracking up. Stig is just standing there, but I'm sure he found it basically pretty funny, 'cos, you know, how couldn't you? It was too, too funny. And poor old Pips, she starts describing her bridesmaid's dress and she's, like, "I don't want to look fat but I want a bit of, you know, *booty.*" Then she says, "I want it to look like that!" and she points at Stiggy's crash helmet. I thought Ems was going to have a seizure at this point. Seriously, it was, like, *beyond* funny. But this guru chappy, he just stares at Stig's head for a minute and then says, "I understand."'

Camilla explains that with a comprehensive programme of yoga, macrobiotics and 'some other cool stuff' in the weeks running up to the Royal Wedding in April 2011, Pippa was able to achieve the precise figure she wanted to best show off her Alexander McQueen bridesmaid's dress. But few knew the inspiration behind her most photographed asset.

'I suppose there was basically only us lot who knew,' Bergman admits. 'But to this day when we see Pips in a pair of white jeans or what-have-you, one of us will always say, "Got Stig's head out today, Pip?" Haaaaaa!'

As for The Stig, is he still part of Pippa's gang? 'Oh, yah, totally part of Pip's crowd,' Camilla confirms, distractedly fiddling with her BlackBerry. 'But, you know, everyone's basically, like, *really* busy these days so we don't see each other so much. But yah, he's around. I suppose he's pretty busy with whatever it is he does? Some sort of PR, I guess. Oh, no, wait, he's on the telly, isn't he? On that show, with the three guys who drive cars and then have an argument about them. Amazing. Anyway, even if The Stig isn't around, we always have Pippa's bottom to remind us of him. Haaaaa!'

I thanked Camilla Bergman for her time and promised we would meet again soon, most likely at the forthcoming launch of Moira Stuart's new range of hats. It was fascinating to hear that The Stig had influenced such an iconic image of modern times, albeit unwittingly. However, I was also fascinated to hear a close-hand tale of his apparent ability to forge friendships, even with someone as unlikely as Pippa Middleton. It seemed to me that it spoke of a softer, more amiable side to The Stig. As I continued my research, however, I began to learn that he is not always that affable. In fact, he is very far from it.

28

BAD MANNERS

In my research so far I had turned up examples of The Stig behaving in a less than pleasant way. His angry response to Scouts seemed reasonable enough given the backstory, but reports that he had tried to destroy Michael Schumacher's private jet with a missile and the physical attack on my person concerned me. Did they hint at some darker side to the man behind the visor? Did his malevolence extend only to those who impersonated him, or was there a wider problem that *Top Gear* team members past and present were politely glossing over, perhaps for fear of losing their jobs or sullying their reputations within the television industry?

I was mulling over this point and getting nowhere with my general enquiries when I received an anonymous approach from someone who claimed to be a former *Top Gear* producer. They referred to themselves only as 'The Whistleblower', although half an hour later they e-mailed back to ask if they could change their codename to 'Mr X', and then sent another message almost immediately requesting that this be altered to 'Commander X'. We exchanged a further seven messages on this matter before agreeing that he would be referred to simply as 'John' since that was his real name and had been in his e-mail address all along. John agreed to meet me in a shadowy car park on the outskirts of Godalming.

I arrived at the allotted time, stepped from my rented Nissan and stood in the cool night air for a few moments. Suddenly, from the very darkest side of the empty tarmac expanse, a single light flashed. I walked towards its source, which turned out to be an ageing Ford Escort with one broken headlamp.

'You weren't followed, were you?' demanded John, as I climbed into the car's passenger side. I assured him that I wasn't and that, besides, I couldn't imagine who would want to follow me to this meeting, anyway.

'You'd be surprised,' John whispered. 'The BBC wants to paint The Stig as this mysterious but harmless hero but, the truth is, he can be a nightmare.'

I'd already heard of The Stig's quirks and foibles, but no-one had been quite so explicit. I asked John to elaborate.

'It's with the star guests, mainly,' John continued. 'That's why *Top Gear* and the Beeb want to keep it on the down low. If it got out just how badly behaved he is with some of the guests, the show would never get another decent star again. I mean, it's hard enough to get them on the show as it is. Think about it, if you go on Graham Norton or Alan Carr, a luxury limo takes you to a nice warm studio in London, you sit on a sofa, have a glass of wine, a funny chat, plug your film, pull a lever to tip a chair over – bosh, you're done. With *Top Gear,* you've got to go all the way down to Surrey, sit in some crummy Portakabin and drive a car around a track as fast as you can. And, if you don't spin off at some point, the production team bully you into going faster until you do because it makes good telly. We were under strict instructions on that one. "Make 'em cry if you have to," we were told, "but make sure they give us a spin or two." It was brutal. I promise you, I saw Cockney hardman Ray Winstone break down right in front of me, blubbing and sobbing, "Please don't make me spin off again!" and the crew going, "Get back in that car, Ray, you scum." Really brutal.'

John reached into the back seat and produced a cylinder of Pringles before continuing: 'So, the guests have to put up with all that stuff, and that's before they even try the catering. Do you remember that big fuss about Patrick Stewart having to pull out of his opening night in *King Lear* in the West End? They said he'd hurt his back during rehearsals for a fight scene, but the truth was he was glued to the bog because he'd been to the *Top Gear* studio and eaten the chicken supreme. Would you like a crisp?'

I declined the offer of a snack but agreed that the *Top Gear* experience sounded like quite an ordeal for star guests.

'Oh, those aren't the worst bits,' John interjected. 'No, the worst thing is The Stig. He's mental.'

I expressed my surprise at this and explained that when I'd seen The Stig working with Matt Smith he had seemed calm and amiable.

'Oh, you must have seen a good one, then,' John muttered through a cloud of Pringle crumbs. 'He probably thinks Doctor Who is real and that he didn't want to mess with an actual Time Lord or something. Like I said, he's mental. I'll give you an example, right? We had Usain Bolt coming on the show and we were all very excited about that. Well, we were just getting the Reasonably Priced Car ready when a new member of the team said, "Just think, the world's fastest man on our show." Big mistake. Stig's standing nearby and you never say something like that when he's nearby. Straight away, I went into damage-limitation mode: "Don't worry, Stig," I said. "He's not fast like you, he's just a runner. You know, running, with your feet ..." and we all start running up and down to demonstrate what running is, but it wasn't getting through. He just stood there with his arms folded for a minute and then walked off. Then Usain Bolt himself arrives and as he's walking over to the track, The Stig comes flying towards him from nowhere and starts trying to stamp on his feet. Now, luckily, Bolt is very laid back so he doesn't react, and we bundle him into the car. But when he gets out after he's done his laps, he falls flat on his face, and then we see that somehow The Stig has tied his shoelaces together. It was embarrassing. One of the world's greatest athletes lying on the ground, and Stig running in circles around him like a loony. We managed to get Bolt to the green room and gave him some lunch, which luckily made him so sick it took his mind off what Stig had done but, even so, it was just rude behaviour on Stig's part.'

This did indeed sound rather petulant. Were there other examples of such silliness with star guests? John paused to pour the remaining Pringle dust down his throat and then assured me that there were.

'It happened loads of times,' he said, wiping around his mouth. 'I'll give you another one – Simon Cowell. First time he came down, he was great. Really fast, seemed to get on well with Stig. But then Stiggy took him out for a fast lap in a Noble, and Cowell was just so cool about the whole thing. Well, Stig might not show any emotion himself but when he takes someone for a hot lap he wants some reaction. Fear, most likely. Like I said, he's mental. But Cowell, his face doesn't change once during the entire lap. So they pull up and, as Cowell gets out, Stig runs up to him and starts trying to stretch and pull his face, you know, trying to get him to pull a different expression or something. It's just crazy. Before we can get to them, they're both on the ground and Stig's still pulling at him and Cowell's shouting, "Arghhh! No! Not my beautiful head!" In the end we had to zap Stig with a cattle prod to get him off. The funny thing is, a lot of it was on camera and when we let Cowell watch the tapes back he really liked how he looked with his skin being pulled tight on his face. Next thing you know, he's had a load of Botox. And he said The Stig incident had given him an idea for a new Saturday night show called *Celebrity Face Fight In A Cage* so actually he was delighted. I gather him and Stig became really good mates.'

As John licked around the top of the Pringles tube, I asked if The Stig was like this with every *Top Gear* guest.

'Oh, no,' John said, quickly. 'He's not always violent. But he can still do stuff that makes them uncomfortable. Like the time Bruce Forsyth came on ...'

I confessed that I didn't remember seeing Bruce Forsyth on *Top Gear* and John was quick to explain why.

'You won't have seen it because it was never broadcast. You see, Bruce comes down to the show, lovely bloke, cracking jokes, doing all the catchphrases and that, but what we didn't know is that The Stig is a massive fan of *Strictly Come Dancing*. I mean, a *massive* fan. And it turns out he thinks he's a bit of a dancer himself. Which is fine, but it also turns out that he can only do the jive. So old Brucie gets into the car on the start line and instead of getting in next to him, Stig just stands next to the driver's window doing the jive. Now Bruce is a pro, so he patiently watches him with a big smile and then applauds, hoping that'll make him stop. But The Stig just carries on. And on. And on. It felt like hours he was at it and, in the end, Stig had jived for so long that Bruce was going to be late to open a new orphanage and we had to let him go.'

I was startled to hear that The Stig had actually prevented guests from appearing on *Top Gear*, and asked John if this happened regularly.

'Not all the time, but it did happen again,' he confirmed. 'Like, you know the girl pop band, The Saturdays? They came down once, and lovely girls they were, too. Now, we always film at the track on a Wednesday and so when we said to The Stig, "Today we've got The Saturdays," he just kept pointing at the calendar in the production office. I said to him, "Don't worry, Stig. It's still a Wednesday. *They're* The Saturdays," but that just made it worse. He started smashing his fist against the calendar and then banging his whole head into it and it didn't help that James May was in the background going, "He's got a point, it is rather confusing ..." and in the end we just had to call the whole thing off before he destroyed the place.'

John pulled a Lion bar from the door pocket of his car, peeled away the wrapper and took an enormous bite.

'You can see why nobody on the *Top Gear* team wants this stuff to get out,' he said, chewily. 'The Stig is basically like a grumpy, spoilt teenager who can't express himself. He just goes about things the way he wants to and sometimes it's a bit embarrassing. I'll give you another example – Peter Jones, the *Dragon's Den* chap. He comes to the car and Stig's got this whiteboard set up next to it with some mad proposal drawn on it for marketing fitness equipment for rats or some bollocks. Well, Jones thinks it's a joke and says something like, "I'll give you 50 grand for 35 per cent of the business." Trouble is, Stig thinks he's serious and, worse than that, I guess he's insulted by this offer 'cos suddenly he starts whacking Peter Jones around the head with this really fat dead rat. Awful behaviour. Really awful.

'But, then again, sometimes he can actually be quite sweet. I remember when we had Sienna Miller as a guest. The thing was, we had grown to suspect that Stig had really got into stage musicals and that his favourite was *Phantom of the Opera*. Makes sense, I suppose: masked man, very misunderstood. I mean, you do the maths. Anyway, Sienna Miller is in the production office waiting for filming to start and she's got to try on this long, black, curly wig for a new role she's playing. Just as she does, Stig comes in, sees her from behind and I suppose he thinks it's Sarah Brightman. Next thing we hear is this right kerfuffle and lots of screaming. Well, Stig has only gone and scooped her up and carried her outside and now he's trying to climb down a manhole with her. She's whacking him and shouting, "Get off me," her agent is there going mad and security are trying to pull Stig out of the manhole. It's just madness.'

John paused to take another bite of Lion bar.

'Of course, some guests don't stand for his nonsense,' John continued, through a ball of wafer, caramel, cereal and chocolate. 'Stephen Fry, for example. Now, he's a clever bloke, as you know, and so it's no surprise that he loves a game of Scrabble. He only has to see the box and he's away, asking if anyone would like a game. Very politely, of course, but he really can't help himself and, as it turns out, there's a Scrabble set in the production office that James May brought in. Well, Fry spots it and asks if anyone would like a game. It's a bit awkward 'cos everyone on the production team is too busy working but we don't want to be rude so when Stig walks past someone says, "Stig, why don't you play Scrabble with Stephen?" You can tell he doesn't really know what's going on but he sits down at this little table in the corner and Fry picks a tile to decide who starts. Well, it's an A so he's straight in there. He picks his letters and then, bless him, he has to help Stig pick his too, without looking, of course – he's too much of a gent to cheat. So then Fry takes his turn and he's straight out of the blocks with a really brainy word. "Litotes" or something like that. Well then, Stig just ignores that word and slaps down a load of letters over the triple word score on one side of the board and what he's put down isn't even a word – it's just XQJWW or something like that. He's basically just used all his high-value tiles. Well, Fry looks at it and says very sweetly, "My dear Stig, that's not strictly a word, you know ..." Next thing, Stig's just flipped the table over in a rage. The board, the letters, the little velvet bag thing, they're all flying across the room. We're about to step in when Fry very calmly stands up, carefully rolls back one cuff on his shirt and punches Stig squarely in the helmet. Well, Stig doesn't know what's hit him – he topples backwards and there he is, lying on the floor with Stephen Fry standing over him. We're all stunned. Then Fry just says something very clever in Latin, "*Et virtus nunc magnit veritas*" or something like that, and calmly strides off. It was amazing.'

If the stories John had told me so far were remarkable, they were nothing to what he was about to reveal, once he had opened a large bottle of Lucozade and taken a series of noisy gulps.

'The problem is, most people don't stand up to The Stig. He's such a loose cannon it's not worth that hassle or the risk of getting hurt. That's basically what happened when the Pope came on.'

I spluttered with surprise. *Top Gear* had invited the Pope to be a guest on the show?

'Oh, yeah. We didn't really have to ask. He was there like a shot,' John confirmed. 'Big car nut, he is. Bit of a front-wheel drive specialist, so he was really looking forward to coming on to do a lap, although officially he was there to promote the Vatican's new range of incense fragranced tissues. Anyway, he turned up as planned but as soon as he got out of his limo The Stig spots him, all done up in the white outfit, and I don't know what happened. He must have thought we were trying to replace him or something, because he grabbed this massive plate of mini Scotch eggs from somewhere and started throwing them full force at His Holiness. Well, that was it – the Pope's security team had him out of there in seconds and we were left without a guest. Again. Thanks a bunch, Stiggy.'

John finished his Lucozade, giving me a moment to take in all the revelations I had just heard. I had been given a big insight into a side of The Stig that I had for some time suspected: that of an unpleasant character with very few social skills.

I left John trying in vain to get his car started so that he could go to McDonald's, and I drove back to London, still working through this rather darker side of The Stig's character.

Of course, in biography writing it's not just people's friends you want to unearth. You can build up a revealing picture by seeking out their enemies too, as I did with my ground-breaking Lady Gaga biography, *Behind The Meat*. Until this work was published, few people realised the scale of her feud with *Last Of The Summer Wine* star, Peter Sallis.

Knowing more about his petulant and nasty side, I started focusing on who The Stig's enemies might be and, aside from Michael Schumacher, another Formula 1 name kept coming to mind. It was time to address the issue of the man that many had told me was The Stig's most hated person in the world.

29

THE RUBENS BARRICHELLO SITUATION

The third episode of *Top Gear's* fifteenth series was very much business as usual. Jeremy Clarkson did some shouting. Richard Hammond got excited about an American car. James May appeared to get lost. But audiences watching this show when it was first transmitted in July 2010 also saw something truly remarkable as, for the first time in history, someone was quicker than The Stig.

That person was Brazilian Formula 1 driver Rubens Barrichello, who piloted the old Suzuki Liana Reasonably Priced Car around the test track a full one-tenth of a second faster than the time recorded by The Stig.

Barrichello was of course delighted and was spotted at a subsequent F1 race in Germany wearing an 'I beat The Stig' T-shirt, which the *Top Gear* presenters, as with everything relating to this matter, treated with customary jocularity. The Stig, however, was less amused.

In the following two weeks, one producer recalls that he was 'almost impossible to deal with', that 'there were bite marks in two metal chairs we left in the office' and that he had 'some high-quality garden furniture delivered to the studio and then kicked the crap out of it'.

Worse yet, there were dark rumours that The Stig continued to exact a dark revenge on Barrichello long after his fury at work appeared to have subsided.

The only way to find out more was to talk to the Brazilian driver. I made contact with his management and was swiftly put in touch with the man himself, e-mailing from his home near São Paulo. I agreed to fly to Brazil and meet with him in person, a complex arrangement that was suddenly overturned when Barrichello remembered he was actually going to be in the UK the following week and perhaps it would be easier to meet there. On the plus side, he would be staying in Surrey which was a lot easier to get to. On the minus side, my flight turned out to be non-refundable.

'Sorry about that,' the F1 veteran said, when we met in the bar of his hotel in Weybridge. 'I actually come to Britain about once a month if I can, partly to catch up with friends but mostly to catch up on *The One Show*. It's so informative. Did you know, maybe as many as 70 per cent of people are on the wrong gas or electricity tariff?'

The Brazilian had the small stature of a typical racing driver but a big, smiling face and a surprising passion for early evening British television. Did he enjoy *Top Gear*, too?

'For sure, *Top Gear* is a great show. Did you know that their office in London is on the floor above *The One Show*? Pretty cool, huh? Oh, man, I love *The One Show*. Did you know there is a vicar in Leicestershire who travels around his village on a unicycle?'

If Barrichello was familiar with *Top Gear*, what was his opinion of The Stig, prior to his time as a guest on the programme?

'For sure, I thought The Stig was a totally cool guy,' the ex-F1 ace enthused. 'I didn't know who he really was but, you know, you could tell he was a great driver. He's quick, he's smooth, he's cool. And he never speaks, right? It reminds me of this thing I saw on *The One Show* about a kid who couldn't talk but he was amazing at math. So, yeah, before I went on *Top Gear*, I had total respect for The Stig, for sure. I respect him like I respect Matt Baker and Alex Jones or, before that, Adrian Chiles and Christine Bleakley.'

Barrichello became side-tracked, speaking at length about a recent *One Show* item on the history of asparagus until eventually I bought him another mineral water from the bar and asked him to talk me through The Stig's reaction to being beaten in the Reasonably Priced Car.

'Actually, at first there was no reaction,' the driver admitted. 'Jeremy revealed the time in the studio and, for sure, I was really pleased, but then I didn't see The Stig again that day. If I had, for sure I would have shaken his hand, even though someone at

From: Rubens Barrichello
To: Simon du Beaumarche
Subject: Re. coming to Brazil

Hi Simon!

I am so pleased you are coming to see me in Brazil. I am a big fan of *Top Gear*! Poweeeer! How I laugh! I look forward to welcoming you to my home.

If you are driving from the airport in São Paulo, here are the directions to reach my house. They are a little complex.

First you want to get out of the airport and take the Rod. President Dutra going east towards Aruja. Follow this for maybe 18 kilometres until you see signs for the exit that takes you to the Rod. Pedro Eroles. Take this road, heading south and in about 5 kilometres it will become the Rod. Professor Alfredo Rolim de Moura. Stay on this road for about 15 kilometres and then get ready to turn right on to Praca Sacadura Cabral and then bear right onto R. Dr Ricardo Viela. Keep your eyes peeled because then you're going to almost immediately turn left onto R. Ten Manoel Alves dos Anjos (it's the second left of two roads, so be careful!) and then less than a kilometre later you turn left again onto R. Ipiranga followed by another right onto R. Joaquim Fabiano de Mello, then immediately first left onto R. Nilo Pecanha. Up ahead you should see a sign for a right turn onto the R. Dom Paulo Rolim Loureiro which you want to take, and then stay on that road for about 10 kilometres until you come to a roundabout.

At the roundabout you're going to take the first exit on the right, onto the SP098 and you're going to follow that for just less than 35 kilometres until you see an exit marked Rod. Dr Manoel Hyppolito Rego. You take that exit and at the bottom of the ramp you go around the roundabout, taking the fourth exit. Next you will come to another roundabout and you want to take the first exit, turning right and then you go across another roundabout and come to a second roundabout where you will turn right onto Avenue Anchieta. Then carry straight on until you see a street called Avenue Dr Raoul Pracatan on the left. Turn here and continue for just less than one kilometre then turn right onto Avenue Ignatio Caphirana de Silva and immediately left again onto an unmarked road which you follow until you see the school on the right, at which point you need to turn left and then follow the road down until a hidden junction on the left. You turn left here and keep driving down until you see a church ahead and a fork in the road. Take the left-hand road and keep driving for maybe 200 metres, then turn right and immediately left under the overhanging tree. Take another left turn at the sign marked 'Angelos' and then right as soon as you can see the top of the barn ahead. My place is the third right after that, round the corner, past the row of trees and the house with the red roof.

Actually, I've just remembered, I'm coming to the UK next week. Maybe we could meet up there instead?

Rubens

Top Gear had warned me never to do that because it would leave purple stuff on your fingers. So I went back to my hotel near Silverstone and, you know, just chilled out and watched *The One Show*. Man, I remember it, they had this great item about a cat that could open cupboards. Crazy! I remember, just after the show ended, there was a knock at my door. So I opened the door and there was a big grandfather clock leaning against it, which fell into the room. If I hadn't jumped out of the way, it would have crushed me! I called reception and asked them not to leave any more grandfather clocks leaning against my door but they didn't seem to know what I was talking about. For sure, it was pretty weird.'

Did Barrichello believe The Stig was responsible for the antiques-based prank at his hotel?

'At the time, I didn't make the connection to The Stig,' he admits. 'If I was going to blame anyone, it would have been Michael Schumacher. We haven't got on since I told him I found *Countdown* boring.'

Barrichello says he put the strange hotel incident to the back of his mind and focused on that weekend's British Grand Prix, but he couldn't ignore the strange and potentially life-threatening things that kept happening.

'I woke up on the Thursday morning and got ready to head to the track for the first practice session,' the Brazilian recalls. 'As I walked down the corridor to reception I heard this noise behind me, looked back and there was a shopping trolley coming towards me, and it had two anvils in it! I managed to jump out of the way at the last minute and you know, if I hadn't, for sure that would have really hurt!'

A perturbed Barrichello drove to the track at Silverstone with his race engineer and tried to think no more of the curious goings-on in his hotel, though when he arrived at the track he found himself in another unusual situation.

'So, I get out of the car at Silverstone and straight away these four or five crows just come from nowhere and start attacking me,' the driver says, with horror. 'It was just crazy! I had to get back in the car and my engineer managed to scare them away with a large umbrella. It was so strange. Why would birds do that? I wanted to call *The One Show* and ask them if they could make an item about random crow attack but, you know, I had a race weekend to focus on first.'

Focus he did, though Barrichello admits the following three days were full of inexplicable incidents and what could be considered at least one attempt on his life: a piano almost fell on him in the hotel car park; a burning arrow was fired at him as he ate dinner; and he returned to his room to find someone had left an extremely angry cow in the bathroom.

'There were so many things, I'm not sure I can remember them all now. All I knew was, for sure, someone was out to get me,' the race ace admits.

On the Sunday evening, after the British Grand Prix was over, the week's *Top Gear* transmitted and the world got to see Barrichello posting his record time in the Reasonably Priced Car.

'It was great!' The Brazilian driver smiles. 'The next day I was at the [Williams F1] factory and all the guys were patting me on the back and congratulating me. For sure, it felt good. But then when I went to leave, I got into my car and just as I was about to drive away, someone opened the back door and released a cloud of wasps into the interior. And they were, like, *really* angry wasps. I jumped out of the car and managed not to get stung but it was a close one. Who would do such a thing? It's crazy. But someone at the factory was looking out of the window at the time and he told me he saw the guy throwing the wasps into the car. He said it was a guy in a white suit and a crash helmet. "Rubens," he said to me, "I think it was The Stig!" Well, I was just, you know, totally confused. Was this guy totally flipping out just because I was one-tenth faster? Wow. Even Eddie Irvine didn't do that. Not much, anyway. It was just totally insane. But, you know, we moved on to the races in Germany and Hungary, it all seemed to go quiet, and then I went back to Brazil for a couple of weeks.'

At the time, Barrichello was yet to realise that, far from giving up on his revenge campaign, The Stig was merely shifting to a more sinister tack. Rather than trying to hurt the Brazilian driver, he started trying to *discredit* him.

'It all started when I was back home in São Paulo,' Barrichello remembers. 'I support an orphanage up in the city, you know, helping out with donations and whatever else I can. So, I've been to the toy store to buy some new toys for the kids and I've wrapped them all up, put them in a big box and written

"From Rubens Barrichello" on the side. A guy comes by with a van and we load the box into the back and it goes off to the city. Later that day I get a call from the manager at the orphanage. She says the box arrived but when they opened it up it did not contain toys. It was full of hornets, bear traps and landmines. Someone had switched the contents. It was a miracle that none of the children was hurt. I was shocked and, straight away, I had an idea of who was responsible for this. It was The Stig. It must have been.'

The campaign against Barrichello continued intermittently for almost a year. F1 team bosses would receive boxes labelled, "Cake! Courtesy of your friend Rubens", but when they opened them, the boxes would actually contain a poisonous snake or large quantity of horse vomit. Car dealers would receive a note saying Rubens Barrichello would be coming to make a personal appearance at their showroom and would advertise the event heavily, drawing a massive crowd of people who would then be attacked by a gang of extremely disgruntled pigs. On one occasion, Barrichello was unknowingly booked onto Brazil's top-rated chat show and, when the host announced him, instead of the beloved racing driver, a mystery figure dressed as a massive hammer with 'Brazil is rubbish' written in Portuguese across it came blundering onto the set and began trying to 'smash' the other guests, the audience and the house band, injuring seven people before evading capture and running away.

In July 2011, however, this campaign of humiliation against Rubens Barrichello suddenly ceased. It is not hard to deduce why. Fellow F1 driver Sebastian Vettel had been a guest on *Top Gear* and had knocked another three-tenths of a second off the Brazilian's already impressive time.

I contacted Vettel's management to see if he, too, had felt the wrath of The Stig after his experience in the Reasonably Priced Car. Their response was terse: 'We cannot discuss The Stig until our investigations are completed,' it said. 'If you have any information about the most recent fire or where the moths are coming from, you must disclose it to us. Otherwise, this matter is closed.'

There was still much about The Stig that was a mystery but one thing was for sure – he does not like to be beaten.

Nor, I must say, do I, and I was starting to become frustrated with my efforts to get to the heart of The Stig. It was time to get serious and attempt to name names.

30

RÄIKKÖSTIG

I had been on the trail of The Stig for over seven months. In that time I had spoken to many expert witnesses, heard from them a multitude of startling revelations, and amassed a wealth of information. However, I was no closer to achieving one of my main goals, which was to reveal his identity. There was nothing for it. It was now time to, as I like to call it, 'go to the wall'. I coined this expression after watching the marvellous television programme *Waking The Dead* and, in particular, the moment in each episode where Trevor Eve gathers his team and they put all the information about the victim – photos, dates, names, clues – on a Perspex wall then try to link everything together to solve the case.

My version of 'going to the wall' is more or less the same, except the wall is the one on the left-hand side of my study rather than in the middle of a pathology laboratory. It is also not made of Perspex since this would compromise its ability to be painted with light grey Farrow & Ball paint to match the rest of the room, and also to support the upper floor of my house.

On this wall I had already pinned all the relevant facts, stories, documents and photos I'd collated on The Stig and I devoted an entire day to simply staring at it, working the evidence over in my mind.

At the end of this day all I had achieved was a shocking headache. It was like being inside a demented maze. Just as I got one plausible thread working, another piece of information would smash into it like an asteroid colliding in outer space and send the whole thing spinning off into a completely different orbit. Who could this one man be, this man that guided history, changed the course of motorsport and may have once punched a horse to the ground?

As daylight gave way to darkness outside I opened a reasonable bottle of Shiraz I had been given by *Masterchef* anchor, Gregg Wallace, in return for helping to get him a Nando's gold card, took a deep breath and decided on another tack. Instead of looking for clues in everything, I would put to one side anything that could be impossible, leaving me with only the possible.

First to go were the presenters' theories. I have no doubt that they themselves believed them, but they were nonsense. Ten years of *Top Gear* had clearly left each of them quite deranged and therefore their elaborate theories could not be trusted. I continued in this vein, stripping away anything that seemed implausible until I was left with a hard kernel of indisputable facts.

Here was a man who was stunningly fast, who hated to talk, who cared not a jot what people thought of his behaviour and who could be as petulant as a child. He had never been paid by the BBC, so he would need his own source of funds. Most important of all, he needed anonymity, to be able to hide away in a place where there were very few people, and where he wouldn't be seen in his white suit. I played around with these thoughts until finally, in the early hours of the morning, I had my eureka moment.

I stood in front of the whiteboard on my *Waking The Dead* wall and looked at what I had written under the heading 'WHO IS THE STIG?' The list was as follows:

- NO TALKING
- OWN MONEY
- SPEED
- EASILY BORED
- NO PEOPLE? WHITE? SNOW … SCANDINAVIA?

At the bottom of the list I slowly wrote the name of the only possible person who tied together all of those things: KIMI RÄIKKÖNEN.

I sat back and drained the last of the Shiraz. All I had to do now was prove my theory beyond doubt …

It was summer. The Formula 1 world was coming to Britain and here I would have my chance to confront Räikkönen himself. I knew it wouldn't be easy but by calling on some contacts I had made within the racing world, I was able to gain access to the paddock at Silverstone on the Thursday before the race.

It was perfect. The place was quiet, save for a few engineers, marketeers and journalists wandering about the long strip of tarmac between the immaculate team hospitality suites and the neat line of lorries directly behind the pit garages themselves. I made my way towards the Lotus facilities and kept watch, waiting for my man to arrive.

My original plan to immediately smoke-out Räikkönen as The Stig had been derailed when it became clear that my paddock pass would not permit me to bring along two Scouts. Instead, I would have to rely on a pointed line of questioning.

At last, my chance came. The air crackles as the drivers arrive, these heroes in garish overalls drawing camera flashes and fawning fans wherever they go, and here, just 20 yards away, a flurry of action signalled the arrival of my target. He was accompanied by just one PR minder, who was expertly batting away questions from some sad hack in a crumpled shirt. I stood my ground until Räikkönen was just feet away. A chubby girl with a rucksack scuttled fearfully towards him, autograph book in hand, nervously conspicuous and conspicuously nervous, competition winner all at sea in an unfamiliar but exciting environment. Kimi didn't even break stride as he left his scrawl on her notepad. Now was my chance. 'Kimi!' I said, loudly.

'No questions at the moment,' snapped the PR man sharply.

'Just one,' I said. 'Kimi, are you The …' I felt a firm grasp on my arm and my body being rotated away from the object of my questioning.

The PR man had seized me: 'Look, mate, I said no questions and that means no questions. You'll get your chance later.' And with that he had followed his driver into the sheeny glass sanctuary of the Lotus motorhome.

I watched other drivers come and go. They seemed happy to answer questions. Why was Kimi so reluctant to face an inquisition? I began to realise that maybe only I knew the real answer to that one. The fewer questions, the less chance of his cover being blown. He was The Stig – I just had to get him to admit it. I skulked around a safe distance from the Lotus facilities. Sooner or later he would have to cross the main thoroughfare to reach the pits and his racing car within, otherwise he would miss today's practice session.

I was almost looking the other way when the time came. At a brisk pace Räikkönen emerged from the motorhome, suited and booted in his full race kit, and headed for the pits. I dashed forwards. 'Kimi!' My cry was ignored.

I began to follow him down the narrow alley between two lorries when a hand clamped onto my shoulder and a voice barked into my ear. 'Not now, mate,' it said. The PR man had caught up with me again. 'I don't think we've met before,' he continued, in a moderately threatening manner. 'Who do you write for, mate?'

I panicked. Not wishing to blow my cover nor mention The Stig before I had a chance to confront Räikkönen, I blurted out the name of the first magazine that came into my head: '*Scouts & Scouting*,' I said.

The PR looked confused for a moment. 'Really? Won a competition or something, did you?' he asked. I nodded. 'Thing is, my friend, Kimi doesn't really like to speak to the press if he can help it. It's nothing personal, just the way he is. You understand, right?'

I smiled weakly. 'I only have one question I want to ask him,' I explained.

The PR man paused for a moment. 'One question? All right, why don't you give me the one question and I'll see if I can get you an answer. How's that?'

Now I was in a bind. Should I ask the real question or field this man a dummy and ambush Räikkönen later? I had to decide fast. 'Erm … could you ask Kimi, was he in the Scouts?'

'That's it?' the PR laughed. 'You're going round the paddock shouting at Kimi and all you want to ask him is if he was in the Scouts? I can tell you now, I'm pretty sure he wasn't, but I'll double-check and get back to you, okay?'

I sensed an opportunity to smoke out The Stig. 'Does Kimi like Scouts?' I added, hopefully.

'Oh, yeah, he thinks they're great,' the PR said briskly, and with that he strode off towards the pit garage.

Something wasn't right. *He thinks they're great.* It sounded sarcastic. It sounded as though, in actual fact, Kimi didn't think Scouts were great at all and that perhaps he had suffered a bad experience with them. This was all too much of a coincidence. I had to act.

I found a place outside the Red Bull hospitality suite from which I could see the TV mounted on the wall inside and watched the practice session take place. As soon as it was drawing to a close I dashed down the paddock to the back of the Lotus pit and lurked behind a lorry cab. Mechanics came and went through the door into the pit itself, but there was no sign of Räikkönen. Eventually, I decided to take matters into my own hands. As a mechanic came out of the door I stepped smartly forwards and walked through it, into the pit garage itself. Almost immediately, I was stopped by a large gentleman with a beard. 'Can I help you?' he drawled.

'I'm here to see Kimi Räikkönen,' I said, confidently.

'He's not here,' the bearded gentlemen replied, firmly.

I looked past the neatly arrayed tool cabinets and stacks of tyres. There, towards the front of the garage, stood a familiar figure. It was Räikkönen. 'Yes, he is,' I said, smoothly. 'He's right over there, now ...' And then everything went dark.

I woke up some hours later in a hotel room, which I later discovered to be in Leicester. This was strange and not a little inconvenient, but at least it told me one thing. Räikkönen was definitely hiding something.

My F1 paddock pass was only good for one day. With no access to the inner sanctum for the rest of the race weekend, I was forced to come up with a new ambush plan. A motorsport contact had told me that in the two-week gap between European races, Räikkönen sometimes retired to a cabin he owned in the wilds of Finland where he could be assured of privacy. My informant was able to give me the name of the nearest village and, with some careful scouting of Google Maps, I was confident

I had located the right place: a cabin by a lake that was conspicuously larger than any other in the area, and which appeared to have a series of circular tracks laid out in the surrounding forest. It was clearly a racing driver's hideaway. I was on the plane to Helsinki the very next day.

I rented a car at the airport and drove over three hours until I reached what appeared to be the right place. The nearest village was nothing more than a small general store, a garage and a cluster of houses. In the workshop of the garage, a man was pushing a new tyre onto a car wheel. 'Excuse me,' I said. 'I'm looking for Kimi Räikkönen.' The man stopped his work, looked up at me and shook his head. He said something in Finnish that sounded extremely unhelpful and then went back to fitting the tyre.

I moved on to the general store. As I walked in, a girl in her twenties was talking to an older lady behind the counter. They both stopped and looked at me. 'Hi, there,' I said. 'I'm looking for Kimi Räikkönen.'

There was a pause. Eventually, the younger woman spoke: 'Looking for Kimi?' she said, flatly. 'Kimi lives in Switzerland.'

'Yes,' I replied. 'But I have heard he has a cabin here, too.'

The girl went to speak but before she could say anything the older lady leapt in: 'Do not look for him!' she blurted.

The first woman shot her a glance. 'She means, you would be wasting your time looking for him here because he does not live in this region,' she said, quickly.

I smiled, thanked the women and left. Something did not add up. I consulted the maps I had printed out at home and decided to head towards what I believed to be the cabin. It was off a long, straight road down a lane that rapidly became a rough, gravelly track through thick pine forests.

As I rounded a gentle right-hand bend through the trees, I came to a large shed in a clearing. Outside, a large man in blue overalls was using an electric saw to cut through tree trunks. As I pulled up, another, smaller figure appeared to run off behind the barn. The first man stopped sawing as I stepped from the car.

'Excuse me,' I said. 'Do you speak English?'

He stared at me for a second. 'No,' he said, firmly. 'I don't speak English.'

'Oh,' I replied. 'Kimi Räikkönen? Here?'

'I told you,' said the man. 'I don't speak any English.'

'Kimi Räikkönen?' I repeated.

'Look,' the man said, gruffly. 'I don't know how many times I can say this, I don't speak English.'

'But … you're speaking English now,' I pointed out.

'These are the only words I know.'

'By coincidence, the words we are using in this conversation are the only words of English you know?'

'That is basically correct.'

'Do you know Kimi Räikkönen?'

'I'm sorry, I can't understand you. I don't speak English.'

I was about to point out the flaws in the man's logic for a second time when from behind the shed there was a sudden blare of engine noise and a loud, off-road motorcycle burst from behind the building and tore past us onto the track heading further into the forest. I knew at once who the rider was. Räikkönen!

'You DO speak English!' I shouted at the man as I leapt into my rented Opel and headed after the motorcycle.

The engine screamed as I drove the car as fast as I dared along the narrow track, thick tree trunks whipping past on both sides. Over the revving of my own machine I was sure I could hear the shrill rasp of the bike as it buzzed deeper and deeper into the thick forest.

I could feel the car slipping and sliding on the track's loose surface and every instinct told me to lift off the accelerator but I couldn't stop now, not with Räikkönen so close and my chance at last to finally answer the question, 'Who is The Stig?'

In my peripheral vision I saw a flash of orange to my left and looked into the dense woodland to see the motorcycle zipping through the trees, its massive, long-travel springs moving up and down as it sped across the uneven forest floor. 'Damn you, Räikkönen!' I shouted out loud as I looked forwards again, just too late to realise I was heading for a sharp left-hand bend in the track. I stamped as hard as I could on the brake pedal, felt it sink to the floor and tingle underfoot as I wrenched the steering wheel left in vain hope of making the turn; but the car slewed sideways and left the track with a thump. There was a loud, dull bang and the car came to a halt.

In a daze I stepped from the driver's seat to survey the damage. The car appeared to have broadsided at least two sturdy pines. As I rounded the front to take in the full extent of the damage I felt suddenly light-headed and fell to the ground. I must have passed out for only a few seconds but when I came to, I was looking up at a very familiar face.

'Hey, are you okay?' it said, flatly.

I blinked twice to focus my eyes. I felt sick and strange, yet I knew that here at last was my chance. 'Kimi,' I gulped. 'Kimi Räikkönen. Are you The Stig?'

He said nothing for a moment. I looked straight into his eyes. They seemed bright, impish and honest.

'No,' he said.

31

THE PROFESSOR

When Kimi Räikkönen told me he was not The Stig, I believed him. In the course of my career I have been lied to by musicians, actors, directors, mime artists, minor royals, major royals and a man who falsely claimed to be Richard Briars. I have developed an instinctive sense for when someone is being honest and, in this case, the mumbling race ace was definitely telling the truth.

A long wait in a Finnish hospital and the flight back to the UK gave me time to reflect on where this left me in my quest to find the truth about The Stig. My conclusion was initially cheery, though this may have been because I had received a blow to the head and been given some painkillers so powerful I had spent 15 minutes inadvertently talking about Catherine Zeta Jones with an oxygen cylinder. When the medication wore off, my assessment of The Stig story so far was significantly less giggly.

Kimi Räikkönen had seemed like the perfect manifestation of so many of The Stig's qualities and I still found it perfectly logical that I had become convinced it must be him inside the white suit. The problem was, now that I knew it wasn't, I struggled to think of anyone else it could be, unless it was a total unknown and, with a man clearly as powerful and talented as The Stig seemed to be, that didn't ring true.

In fact, many things didn't ring true, not least his apparent involvement in world events stretching back over half a century. Either there were generations of Stigs – if so, who were their mothers and how was this lineage concealed from public records? – or all of these achievements could be ascribed to The Stig himself, in which case I would estimate him to be at least 60 years old. It just didn't add up.

The question of age was at the top of a spider diagram of thoughts and questions that I sketched in my notebook on the aeroplane home. To cheer myself up, I drew an actual spider in the top left-hand corner. It didn't help.

As the plane touched down at Heathrow Airport I stared at the key words and phrases on the page again: 'ageless', 'powerful', 'supreme ability', 'tireless', 'Surrey'. Just as we arrived at the terminal and the captain requested that the cabin doors be set to manual, the answer struck me.

My God, why had I never given this serious thought before, when it now seemed so logical? The Stig was a complex humanoid robot! All those jocular studio introductions Jeremy Clarkson had made on *Top Gear*, they were actually allusions to the truth! The Stig did have hydraulic legs! His heart did tick like a watch! He did have a digital face! These were not jokes;

they were clues! Suddenly everything was falling into place. The only question was, where did this insanely futuristic mechanoid come from? Someone must have made him and released him into the world. In the taxi back to my home, I stared again at the diagram until one word rang out with bell-like clarity as the answer to this knotty question: 'Surrey'.

I had realised some time ago that almost everything in my search for the real Stig had led to Surrey (apart from the bit in Finland, obviously), and there was only one man I knew in the whole of Surrey who was capable of creating such a forward-thinking, radical and highly advanced robot. One of the most celebrated Formula 1 designers of all time, a man for whom the word 'genius' was not an understatement, a man who had set new benchmarks in racing cars, who had created world championship-winning machines for driving legends such as Alain Prost and Ayrton Senna, and who went on to create a new benchmark in road cars with the legendary McLaren F1 supercar – Professor Gordon Murray.

Everything started to make sense. Murray had the technical skills, he had the history of left-field thinking, he lived near Godalming. It had to be him! The Stig had to be some remnant of a top-secret project to create the perfect Formula 1 driver. Murray, ever the perfectionist, had clearly realised that drivers were the one weak, inconsistent link in his otherwise flawless F1 car designs, and he had come up with a way to make them as perfect as the rest of his engineering; but the motorsport authorities, mindful that even the tiny personalities of racing drivers were better than no personality at all, had banned his creation before it was even made public, and the poor redundant robot was purchased by the BBC who used it on *Top Gear* whilst creating an elaborate, scripted smoke screen around it to prevent the controversial truth from leaking out. It all sounded so plausible as I mulled it over in my head; I just needed to get confirmation from the horse's mouth.

Using my contacts in the F1 world I was able to find out precisely where Murray lived and decided to take radical action. Setting up an interview by phone would only risk rejection or stonewalling: clearly The Stig was something that Murray did not want to be identified with, and the only way to get him to admit the existence of this mind-boggling project was to confront him directly and without warning.

I rented another car, drove down to Surrey and parked in a leafy lane close to Murray's address, before walking briskly down the road and up the drive that led to his large, secluded house. I knocked firmly on the weathered, wooden front door, my heart pounding in my chest, and almost instantly heard someone operating the latch on the other side.

The door swung open and there stood Murray himself, a tall man in a luridly patterned shirt, his face defined by the long hair lapping over his collar and the trademark bristly moustache on his top lip. This was no time for pleasantries; I had to dive straight in. 'I know the secret, Gordon!' I said, stridently. 'I know!'

He looked taken aback and then almost immediately crestfallen. 'Okay, okay,' he muttered, softly. 'You've got me. You've got me. Yes, it's false. The moustache is false. Always has been. I just thought it looked cool ...'

There was a moment of confused silence. I broke it with another accusatory statement. 'Not that,' I barked. 'The Stig! I know about you and The Stig! I know he's a robot you created in order to make the perfect racing driver!'

Murray looked genuinely confused. 'Wow!' he said quietly, after a brief pause. 'I've never been accused of that before.'

Breathlessly, I told him I was writing a book about The Stig, that I had compiled a vast body of research and that this was the only possible conclusion. Murray furrowed his brow. 'I think we need to straighten this one out,' he said evenly and then, to my surprise, he gestured for me to come in to his house.

We settled in an airy sitting room at the back of the house, the walls adorned with Bob Dylan posters and the large French doors affording an excellent view of the sweeping lawn beyond. I declined Murray's offer of a drink or something to eat and sat down on a large sofa facing the windows. Murray settled in an armchair at 90 degrees to me and slowly opened a bag of Quavers. 'My favourite crisps,' he noted. 'They're so light.'

He munched on a handful of the cheesy snacks then set the bag down on a side table and fixed me with a steely gaze. 'So,' he said carefully, in his soft, measured voice. 'You think I engineered a fully functioning humanoid robot that can reliably and consistently drive a car to the furthest extremes of its performance envelope and is capable of a complex assimilation of human behaviour?'

I confirmed that this was precisely what I believed. Murray took another mouthful of crisps and then slowly peeled off his moustache. 'Might as well take that off, since you know.' He smiled. 'Saves getting crumbs in it.'

He removed a small carbon-fibre case from his pocket, placed the stick-on moustache inside and then set the case down on the table beside him before turning back to face me.

'Well, I'm very flattered that you think I would be capable of designing something of that nature and making it work,' he said, with a wry smile. 'Here, let me show you something ...' He reached into a magazine rack beside his chair from which he plucked a copy of a magazine called *Complicated Engineering*, thumbing through it until he reached a specific article which he then handed to me. It was about a white, two-legged, vaguely human-shaped robot called ASIMO that had been built by Honda in Japan.

'Honda has been working on this technology since the 1980s,' Murray observed. 'And they're still only at the point where it can do things we take for granted like climbing stairs or picking up a cup. Now, that's with all the money and man-power of Honda behind it. And you think that I could come up with something significantly more advanced than that, working alone or with a small team? I wish I could, but I'm afraid it's simply not possible.'

Murray had a point. But I had a second theory that I put to him at this point: The Stig was half-human, half-robot. His legs were indeed hydraulic, but they were attached to a torso of real flesh and blood and controlled by the most advanced computer in the world, the human brain.

Murray chuckled again before taking another couple of Quavers and feeding them into his mouth.

'Again, I'm delighted that you think I would be capable of engineering such a thing,' he said, sweetly. 'And you're right, such technology does exist in the form of bionic limbs for amputees that can be controlled by nerve impulses. But the level of control is relatively rudimentary at this point, and it's not something I have any experience in designing, never mind installing on an actual person. I'm an engineer not a doctor, Simon ... Are you okay?'

In truth, I was not. I had spent almost a year of my life researching The Stig, watching hours of *Top Gear*, reading hundreds of books and magazine articles, talking to dozens of people, and all for what? I had come up with new and ever more elaborate theories to explain The Stig enigma and each one had been torn down in front of me. Once again, I felt no closer to the truth than I had been when I first agreed to write this book and now, sitting in Gordon Murray's house listening to his calm and rational explanations for why The Stig was not a partial or full mechanoid, I suddenly felt like this had all been a total waste of time.

I stared blankly out of the French doors until Murray once again asked if I was okay. I'm embarrassed to say that, without thinking, I vented many of my frustrations, about the hours of wasted research, the inconclusive stories, the frustrating dead ends and the ludicrous theories about super-soldiers.

'Oh, yes, the super-soldiers. I've heard that one,' Murray smirked. 'But the truth is, The Stig isn't a robot or an alien life form. He's not the product of intercourse on Concorde or the son of a legendary horse trainer, and he's certainly not a super-soldier from a secret American military project.'

Murray finished the last of his Quavers and carefully folded the empty packet in on itself to form a small, yellow square, which he set down on the table beside his armchair. He cleared his throat and continued: 'Maybe people believe what they want to believe,' he said, softly. 'As with so many things in life, they want the background story to be to be bizarre and complicated. But the truth? Well that's very, very simple ...'

Murray picked up a notepad and pen from the side table, quickly scribbled something down, tore off the top page, folded it over and handed it to me.

'That should give you what you're looking for.' Murray smiled enigmatically and with that he stood up, ushering me graciously but firmly towards the door before I could unfold the paper to see what was written upon it.

Only when I was outside Murray's house did I have the chance to see what he had inscribed on this small sheet of note paper. It was just three words and a number: '29 Magnolia Avenue, Guildford'. Underneath he'd drawn a little smiley face, which I thought was rather out of character.

I considered knocking on the door again to ask for more information, but I felt awkward troubling Prof. Gordon Murray again. He had given me enough. In this thankless quest to find out anything concrete about The Stig, I had nothing to lose by turning my attentions to what lay at 29 Magnolia Avenue, Guildford.

32

29 MAGNOLIA AVENUE

There was no time to engage in further research. I had been given an address and a suggestion that it would hold the key to all that I sought to find out about The Stig. My next move was simple – I would drive to this address and see what it held. I walked briskly up the lane from Gordon Murray's house, jumped into my rented Renault and headed straight for 29 Magnolia Avenue, Guildford.

The drive must have taken barely more than 20 minutes yet, in truth, I didn't register the time for my mind was consumed with curiosity at what I would find at this address. My satellite navigation guided me around the centre of Guildford, onto a main road leading north and then suddenly right, into an estate of new-build houses on the outskirts of the town. I would guess the estate was no more than two or three years old, the properties still bright of brickwork and green of lawn in that sheeny, slightly soulless style that new construction brings. The second road on the left was Magnolia Avenue. I turned into the street and drove slowly down its smooth tarmac, peering at the house numbers until eventually I found what I was looking for. Number 29.

It was a semi-detached house in the same blandly simple style as the rest of the development, with a single bay window and a white painted front door on the ground floor and two windows on the upper floor; each detail almost perfectly mirrored by the conjoined house to its right. The driveway sloped upwards slightly from the road and led to a garage, set back slightly from the front of the house on the left. It was, all told, an unremarkable house on an unremarkable street. I began to think that Gordon Murray had made a mistake or, worse still, had deliberately sent me on a wild goose chase.

I turned around further down the street and parked diagonally opposite number 29, in front of some bushes and the entrance to a path that cut through to an adjacent road. Stepping from my car, the street seemed very quiet. I walked smartly across the road, up the driveway of number 29, onto the path that cut into the small front lawn and up to the front door. I hesitated for a moment and then jabbed nervously at the brass-effect doorbell button on the right-hand doorframe. Inside the house I heard a synthesised chime and then … nothing. The lack of sound and movement inside the house only seemed to amplify the strange quiet on the street outside. I pushed the doorbell button once again and heard the same digitised bell sound, which faded into the same heavy silence. Clearly there was no-one home.

Glancing back at the street behind me, I could see no sign of human life and, at the risk of looking furtive, I stepped slowly onto the lawn so as to peer in through the bay window to my right. It was dark inside but I could make out a cream leather sofa up against the back wall of the room beneath an unremarkable print of some sunflowers. On the wall to the right was a pale marble-effect fireplace with a small gold clock on its mantle and a rectangular mirror hanging above it. It looked like a very ordinary sitting room in a very ordinary house. Surely this couldn't provide the answer to anything?

Before I aroused suspicion, I walked briskly away from the house and back to my car. What to do now? I settled into the driver's seat but did not start the engine, deciding instead to watch the house for a while in the hope that its occupant(s) would return.

After 20 minutes or so, a blue car drove past and I watched in the rear-view mirror as it turned into a driveway some seven or eight houses down. Thirty-five minutes after that, a man walked past with a fat Labrador. Nothing else happened. That is until 6.58 p.m., when a grey Toyota Yaris drove slowly down the road towards me and pulled into the driveway of 29 Magnolia Avenue. The reversing lights flashed briefly as it came to a stop, leading me to believe the car had an automatic gearbox. It was a gloomy evening and I saw the interior light come on as the driver's door opened. Then, from my vantage point across the street, I watched as a smooth, rounded, white shape rose up above the Toyota's roof. The driver was wearing a white crash helmet. It was him. It was The Stig.

My first instinct was to leap from the car and run up the driveway to confront him, but I swiftly thought better of it and instead I watched as he closed the door of the Toyota, carefully pressed the button on the key until the indicators flashed to acknowledge that the car was locked, and then trudged up to the white front door and let himself into the house. He was carrying an unbranded carrier bag and his body language seemed a little careworn, but it was definitely him. It was definitely The Stig, and he had definitely just walked into a new-build semi-detached house on the outskirts of Guildford as if it was his own.

I kept watching the house. A man emerged from a property some three houses down on the right and dragged a wheelie bin to the end of his driveway. Exactly 17 minutes later another neighbour did likewise. No-one disturbed me in my car parked across the street. At 8.52 p.m. a light went on in the downstairs window at number 29 and there he was again, still in his white suit and crash helmet. He walked to the window and lowered a frilly Roman blind. Then all was still.

I was just considering my next move when the light next to the front door flicked on and the door itself slowly opened. The Stig was coming out of the house, still dressed in his trademark helmet, suit and racing boots. He was carrying a black rubbish bag, which he took around the side of the house and dumped into a black wheelie bin. He then dragged the wheelie bin down the drive, past the grey Toyota, and left it at the edge of the pavement. He walked back into the house but left the front door open. With the lights on inside I could see a small sliver of the hallway. It appeared to be painted an unremarkable cream colour and there was what looked like a framed generic photograph of a sunset on the wall. Suddenly, The Stig re-emerged carrying a purple box, which he placed next to the wheelie bin at the end of the drive before returning to the house and emerging once more, this time with a green box that he neatly set down beside its more brightly coloured compatriot. This, I guessed, was his recycling. With that done, he walked back into the house and closed the front door.

I waited for a good half-hour, then stepped quietly from my car and walked towards 29 Magnolia Avenue. It was approaching 10 p.m. on this dismal early September evening and the sky was now dark, the broadly spaced streetlights providing scant illumination of the pavements below.

I stopped to look into the recycling bins The Stig had left out for collection. In the purple box he had neatly sorted all his cardboard and paper. Poking at the contents told me little, except that he ate Kellogg's variety pack miniature cereal boxes and got through a reasonable amount of lavatory paper, though nothing that I could truly call 'above average'. In the green box was a tin of oxtail soup, several empty pots of Fruits Of The Forest yoghurt and a used can of Lynx 'Sport Blast' deodorant. In all, nothing out of the ordinary.

I looked around to make sure there was no-one on the street and then crept up the driveway, past the front door and stopped nervously next to the downstairs bay window. Through the blind I could see the flickering light of a television. I eased myself slowly closer to the side of the window and peered through the gap between the blind and the wall inside. There was The Stig, sitting on the sofa. He appeared to be intently watching a large TV, the back of which I could just see to the right before the silvery fabric of the blind encroached on my view. I held my breath as I strained to hear the sound from the television, curious to know what it was that held The Stig's attention so keenly. There were voices but they were muffled and indistinct. Moments later, they gave way to a theme tune, presumably over some closing credits. I recognised the music. It was from the popular ITV *Inspector Morse* spin-off, *Lewis.*

As the programme ended, The Stig stayed in his seat. Through the damping effect of the window I could hear the bright, attention-grabbing sounds of adverts playing. The Stig made no effort to change the channel. Instead, he reached onto the table beside the sofa, picked up a mobile phone, glanced quickly at the screen and then placed it back where it had been. Another muffled but familiar theme tune began: the strident, percussive sound that introduced ITV's *News At Ten*. The Stig remained where he was, inert on the sofa. I crept slowly away before I was spotted acting in this bizarre and intrusive manner.

I got back into my car and sat for a moment staring at the house. It was all deeply unremarkable. Everything about The

Stig's life at 29 Magnolia Avenue seemed unremarkable. His house, his car, his décor, his recycling, his evening in with a drama series and then the 10 o'clock news.

Was this it? Was this what lay behind the ludicrous stories of secret army projects, the imaginative claims of bizarre appetites and the jocular references to sleeping in a tree? It wasn't that The Stig was strange and unusual at all. Based on what I had seen this evening, he was actually shockingly boring.

I was about to drive home to ponder my next move when something prompted me to have one last poke into The Stig's seemingly mundane existence. I calmly crossed the street again to the wheelie bin, opened the lid, yanked the carefully tied black sack from within and strode smoothly back down the drive and diagonally across the street to the car. I was standing by the boot, struggling in the darkness to see the button on the key that would release its latch, when I heard a car coming down the street from behind me and I panicked, throwing the bag into the bushes that framed the path entrance. I turned around just as the approaching vehicle, a dark-coloured Audi TT, rounded the gentle curve in Magnolia Avenue, its headlights cutting through the blue gloom of night with an icy glare. The car drove past me without stopping and I watched as it continued towards the end of the road and turned to head out of the estate.

As soon as it disappeared from view, I turned and was about to step up onto the kerb when a gruff voice spoke out, making me jump out of my skin. 'Can I help you?' it said, firmly.

I looked around to see over the Renault's roof a man approaching from across the street. From the angle of his approach, I guessed that he lived in the house next door to The Stig's.

'I said, can I help you?' the man repeated. He was in his late fifties, tall, thickset and with the faintly threatening air of a pub landlord.

'No, thank you,' I said, moving towards the driver's door.

'What are you hanging about here for at this time of night?' the man demanded. His tone was confrontational, his accent northern.

I said nothing but opened the car door.

'Can you hear me, son?' the man barked, sounding angrier with every utterance. 'Do you want me to call the police?'

'I am police,' I replied unconvincingly, clumsily dropping the definite article. Without waiting to hear his response I slid quickly into the driver's seat, slammed the door and jabbed the dashboard button marked START. As soon as the engine fired I slotted the car into gear and sped away.

Safely back at home, I barely slept that night as I considered what I had seen. As the evidence swirled around and around in my head, I could reach only one conclusion: The Stig was not strange and mysterious and exciting. All those comical introductions and amusing television set pieces, they were all confected to make him seem interesting when, in fact, the exact opposite was true; and tonight I had unearthed that truth. There in that ordinary street in that ordinary house as I saw him doing ordinary things I had exposed the greatest secret of them all – The Stig is actually extremely boring.

I was shaken by this revelation but not so shaken I could not give serious thought to my next move. I had no doubt that getting out of Magnolia Avenue when I did was the right thing: I had no desire to cause a disturbance, nor get the police involved, especially as either could have alerted The Stig to my presence before I had had time to calculate the best way to approach him.

Many hours of staring at the ceiling later, I concluded that monitoring the house again would yield little progress. I was likely only to see the same mundane comings and goings, with no further insight into The Stig's character. Plus, the angry northern man from the house next door would be sure to notice me on such a quiet street, leading to another unwanted altercation. No, the only real course of action left to me was to return to Guildford and knock on The Stig's door, and it seemed to me there was no time like the present.

I left my house at just after 6 a.m. and drove briskly through the awakening streets of London, down onto the A3 and straight into Surrey. I was turning into Magnolia Avenue by 7.40 a.m.

During my nocturnal planning, I had considered leaving the car several houses away, reasoning that an approach on foot would be quieter and therefore give me the element of surprise. However, I began to consider a worst-case scenario in which some unspecified problem – attack from angry northern neighbour, attack from The Stig himself – might require me to make a fast getaway and, for that reason, I had decided to park directly outside number 29. Accordingly, I pulled up outside, shut off the engine the instant I came to a halt and in one smooth motion yanked on the door release and stepped from the car.

Straight away, I noticed that the house looked different. For one thing, the grey Toyota was not on the driveway as it had been last night. Curses! If The Stig had already gone out I would be forced to leave the immediate area and take my chances coming back later to catch him at home. Yet the absence of a car on the drive was not the only difference. The wheelie bin and the recycling boxes were no longer at the end of the driveway, even though a glance down the street showed that these items were still at the end of each neighbour's drive and they appeared to be full. If the dustmen had not yet made their rounds, why had The Stig taken in his rubbish?

As I walked up the drive I noticed that the blind was no longer down in the sitting room window and nor were curtains drawn in the upstairs windows. I stopped at the front door and without hesitation prodded firmly on the doorbell button, expecting to hear the digital chimes ringing inside. Instead, there was only silence. I pressed the button again and still no sound could be heard. It seemed curious that the batteries had failed between yesterday evening and now, but I had no time to dwell on this and instead rapped as loudly as I dared on the wooden front door itself. There was no response. No sound, no switching on of lights, no sense of movement whatsoever.

I stepped to the right and peered in through the sitting room window. The sight that greeted me was such a shock that I exclaimed an expletive under my breath.

The room was completely empty. The sofa, the television, the picture, the mirror, the clock on the mantelpiece; they were all gone, leaving just a bare, empty space. The place had been cleared.

I stepped back onto the drive and approached the tall wooden gate between the house and the garage, giving it a gentle push which, to my surprise, caused it to swing open, revealing a path turning right around the back of the house and a tufty lawn to the rear. I followed the path and looked into the first window I arrived at, finding myself gazing in on a bare kitchen, devoid of the appliances and trinkets that normally infest the work surfaces in a populated house. The other downstairs window was a large sliding patio door and it, too, gave sight only of a bare, white-walled space utterly barren but for a single light bulb hanging from the ceiling.

This was absurd. Less than ten hours earlier I had seen The Stig occupying this very house and caught glimpses of furniture and decoration that told me this was someone's home. Now, inexplicably, the place was empty of people, of trimmings, of life.

I didn't know what to think any more. Had The Stig realised that I was on to him and bolted? It was possible, but why would he strip his house of all possessions? Come to that, *how* would he do such a thing, especially in such a short time, in the dead of night and given that he appeared to drive a rather small car?

I paced back and forth on the path at the back of the empty house until, suddenly, the penny dropped. *Top Gear* had invested a great deal of time and effort in creating and maintaining the mystique of The Stig. It was in their interests to see that this myth was never destroyed by someone discovering the rather anodyne truth about the tame racing driver's simple suburban existence. Of course one man could not disappear into the night and take the contents of an entire house with him, but with the might and manpower of the BBC on his side, anything was possible.

It seemed clear that as soon as The Stig had got wind that someone had tracked him down to Magnolia Avenue, he activated some carefully arranged *Top Gear* emergency plan that would extract him from his small, semi-detached house and leave no trace that he had ever lived there. Well, it was too late now, Stig; I was on to you.

I pulled out my mobile phone and scrolled through the numbers. It was time to take this to the very top. I couldn't ring The Stig himself but I could call *Top Gear* executive production director, Adam Milwyn, and challenge him with my findings. Milwyn had declined to be interviewed for this book but had happily given me his number and cheerfully lent assistance with visits to the studio, interviews with presenters and so on. Now it was time to confront him with the truth that he and his team, past and present, had so carefully tried to keep from me.

I selected Milwyn's number and pressed the phone to my ear as the ringing sound started in the ear piece. After four rings, a gruff voice answered with a single, 'Yes?'

'Adam, it's Simon du Beaumarche,' I began.

'What?' he grunted.

'Simon du Beaumarche, the biographer,' I continued.

'Oh, right. Hello,' Milwyn said, cautiously.

'Adam, I've discovered something about The Stig and I wondered if you could comment on it,' I said, briskly. 'I have discovered conclusively that he lives in a new-build, semi-detached house on a development in Guildford, he drives a grey Toyota Yaris and he lives a very normal life which you and *Top Gear* are covering up at any cost so as to make the TV character of The Stig seem interesting and quirky so that people will keep watching your show and buying related items of merchandise. Am I right?'

There was a muffled snort down the line. 'The Stig? In a what? A new-build semi?' Milwyn laughed. 'You're having me on, mate. That's ridiculous. The Stig lives in, I don't know, a tree or something. Yeah, he sleeps upside-down like a bat. Don't you watch the show?'

'I have watched the show, Adam,' I replied. 'And I know all about your ongoing attempts to paint this man as eccentric and odd, but it just won't wash. I've seen him going into a very ordinary house, I've seen him put out his recycling, I've seen him watching TV. I've seen him being *boring*.'

'You've got a good imagination, mate, I'll give you that,' Milwyn said, in a slightly patronising tone.

'There's no imagination necessary, Adam,' I replied, firmly. 'I saw these things with my own eyes only last night. The funny thing is, I'm standing at the back of the house right now and, guess what? It's completely empty. Overnight some person, or some organisation, has stripped this house and attempted to make it look like The Stig never lived here. But he did, Adam. I saw him.'

'No, mate,' Milwyn said, suddenly sounding angry. 'You saw nothing,' and with that he hung up.

I stood in the garden for a moment taking deep drags of the cool morning air, before walking back around the side of the house and returning to my car. What to do next? Milwyn was clearly rattled by my findings, and that was surely proof that what I had discovered was the truth. A rather disappointing truth, but the truth nonetheless.

Ideally, I needed to track down The Stig. I presumed he would find a new 'safe house', but finding him and it would be incredibly difficult. There were many new developments in the Guildford area alone, and I couldn't very well cruise around all of them in the hope of spotting him mowing his lawn or repainting his garage door. It would be pointless waiting for a new phone book to be published since I presumed he would be ex-directory. For now, I was resigned to returning home and typing up what I knew so far.

I was about to drive off when suddenly I remembered one thing. The bin bag! In my panic last night I had thrown it into the bushes by the path entrance diagonally opposite The Stig's house, but it had been dark, the angry northern neighbour appeared not to have seen me do it and the rubbish collectors had not yet made their rounds. It would surely lead to nothing, but it was worth checking, if only to find more reassurance that my theory about Boring Stig was correct. I waited for a silver Volkswagen to pass down the street and then ran across the road and towards the bushes.

I looked down into the long grass at the entrance to the pathway and there it was: an oily black shape glistening with blobs of morning dew amongst the damp, verdant undergrowth. I grabbed the bag, walked quickly back to the car and avoided another delay with the boot by dumping it straight onto the back seat. I took one last look at 29 Magnolia Avenue and drove away.

The morning rush hour getting into London is no time to have a rather fragrant bag of household rubbish on your back seat, but I eventually made it home and with only a small amount of gagging. As soon as I pulled up, I yanked the damp bag from the car and carried it briskly through the house to my garden, pausing only to grab a large knife from the kitchen.

Once outdoors again I made a vigorous slash in the dark skin of the bag and ripped it open to gaze upon its contents. I was not prepared for what lay before me, and I felt myself involuntarily shudder as I looked upon the items now strewn on my decking. The tally of items in the bag was as follows: seven empty tubs of mint choc chip ice cream, 32 packets of macaroni cheese mix, nine jagged pieces of balsa wood, a half-empty bottle of squid ink, 19 empty jars of Bovril, a jar of mint sauce that now contained a thick, orangey liquid, a crumpled picture of Janet Jackson from the early 1990s, a dismembered clock radio alarm with bite marks in the casing, a small, empty metal box with a 'Hazardous waste' sticker on it, the CD booklet from the Take That album *The Circus* with Mark Owen's head cut out from the front, a compliments slip which appeared to be from the office of the President of the United States with '*Thanks! B*' written on it, and a dead blackbird with a Post-it note stapled to its side that appeared to bear the word 'Keith'.

This was not normal rubbish. It was strange and unsettling rubbish containing the kind of items only an eccentric, erratic, possibly unhinged character would throw out. I don't mind admitting that I was shaken, and not just because the contents of the black bag smelt quite extraordinarily bad.

My first thought was that I had been set up, that the same *Top Gear* team that had 'swept' the house on Magnolia Avenue had planted this rubbish so that I might find it and believe The Stig was still the quirky character of legend. Yet, logically, it seemed highly unlikely that this was possible. No-one had seen me throw the bag into the bushes the night before. As far as the people charged with covering up for The Stig were concerned, this was 'off the radar', a piece of evidence they knew nothing about and which would have evaded their otherwise seamless operation to banish all signs of life from number 29. What I had here was something that had slipped through the cracks. More than that, I had something that confirmed what I had suspected about the man I had been pursuing for the past year. He wasn't boring after all. Here, strewn outside my French doors, I had concrete evidence that despite the utter normality of his suburban surroundings, my target was still strange, mysterious, unique and unfathomable. He was still The Stig.

CONCLUSION

With a publication deadline looming, I was reaching the end of my quest to find the truth about The Stig. I had met dozens of people, heard countless stories and, during work on a chapter that was subsequently pulled for legal reasons, become embroiled in a rather unusual brawl with the actor, Nigel Havers.

It had been a fascinating journey, full of twists and turns and a well-known British actor calling me a 'cockface'. One thing that I had concluded on this epic voyage of discovery is that The Stig, whoever he is, seems to have touched a great number of lives and that his influence stretches across many decades, many continents and many key moments in politics, industry and the arts. It would be fair to say that The Stig has been a powerful force within history itself.

However, the moment when I discovered him living in a very normal house in a very normal street in Surrey was a severe blow, since it seemed to suggest that he was not the dynamic and unusual person I had been led to believe. I began to feel that *Top Gear* had created this character through their television programme and were now using me to write a book that would perpetuate the myth built up on TV. That, in turn, cast doubts upon the many wonderful stories I had heard as I started to fear that they were all carefully constructed and cunningly planted to make me – and therefore the loyal *Top Gear* audience – believe what they wanted us to believe about The Stig, when in truth he was extremely ordinary and boring.

That would have been the disappointing end to my quest had it not been for the bizarre bag of rubbish that I had secured without *Top Gear*'s knowledge. This was unsolicited evidence that spoke volumes about the man behind the visor. The items in his rubbish immediately proved to me that, for better or worse, The Stig is not like other people. He is strange, yes, but he is also unique. Only a person so left-field and single minded would be able to invent punk, engineer the Mini, inspire great artworks, influence motor-racing heroes and bring about political change across Europe. He isn't boring at all: he is a ground-breaker, a powerhouse, a force of nature. He is a hero.

Kara, this is as far as I've got with the conclusion. Was hoping to finish it today but I've just unearthed some very interesting additional information that may require a substantial re-write. Will update you as soon as possible. SdB

On Friday 3 August 2012, Simon du Beaumarche e-mailed the words you have read in this chapter to my office, as he had been doing regularly with the other chapters for this book ever since he started writing it. The document was accompanied by an updated list of those he wished to thank in the acknowledgements section, and a note saying he would have more material, including a revised introduction, on Monday morning. These updates never arrived.

On Monday evening, I rang Simon to make sure that everything was okay. His mobile phone appeared to be switched off and there was no reply from the landline at his house in North London, where he lived alone. The same was true when I called again on Tuesday, Wednesday and Thursday. Concerned for his wellbeing, I drove to his house on the Thursday evening and received no answer when I rang the doorbell. A neighbour noticed me waiting outside and asked if she could help. After the situation was explained, she confessed that she had not seen Simon all week but that she had a spare key to his front door and would accompany me into the house to make sure nothing was amiss.

I had visited Simon at home many times over the years and, when we entered the house, everything seemed familiar, giving no cause for alarm. The place was clean and tidy. There was no sign of a break-in. There was also no sign of Simon himself. Only the condition of his home office aroused suspicion. I knew from previous visits that Simon worked on an Apple iMac desktop computer that sat on a large, darkwood desk against the far wall of the room. The computer was no longer there. On the left-hand side of the office was the wall upon which Simon would pin pictures, notes and other pieces of relevant information about his latest subject. Every time I had been in this room, the wall had been festooned with paper, yet that day it was completely bare. There were files in a row on a shelf to the right, each marked with a familiar name: 'Jeremy Kyle', 'Carol Thatcher', 'That bastard Nigel Havers'. It struck me that I couldn't see a single file relating to The Stig there or anywhere else in the house. Using the phone on Simon's desk I tried once more to call his mobile. It was still switched off.

The following morning we alerted the police to his disappearance. They discovered that he last used his debit card to buy a bottle of wine and some langoustines from a local supermarket on the evening of Friday 3 August, the same day I last heard from him. There have been no transactions on any of his bank cards and no sightings of him in his neighbourhood since that day.

As the time of writing, we have still not heard from Simon. We are publishing this, one of his greatest works to date, as a tribute to a wonderful writer, a fine biographer and a true friend, in the hope that it may prompt him, or someone close to him, to let us know he is safe.

If you have any information about his whereabouts, then please let us know by email at findsimon@randomhouse.co.uk.

Kara Elms
Publisher
London, October 2012

ACKNOWLEDGEMENTS

Many people have given me support, directly or indirectly, during the writing of this book. It would be impossible to thank them all individually but I would like to give special mention to the following:

The Earl of Westerchester, Patti LaBelle, Eddie Large, Anita Dobson, Mollington Dogg, Steve Davis, Freshways dry cleaner, Hats of Holloway, Danny and all at The Cappuccino Yurt, Sir William R, Sir William S, Sir William T and the Dimblebys.

I would also like to offer sincere thanks to Alex Renton, Greg Vince, Julianna Porter, Lorna Russell, Joe Cottington, the ever-patient Kara Elms and especially to Andy Wilman. Finally, thank you to Richard Porter without whom this would not have been possible.

INDEX